# POPPY

Reaktion's Botanical series is the first of its kind, integrating horticultural and botanical writing with a broader account of the cultural and social impact of trees, plants and flowers.

*Published*

*Apple* Marcia Reiss
*Bamboo* Susanne Lucas
*Cannabis* Chris Duvall
*Carnation* Twigs Way
*Geranium* Kasia Boddy
*Grasses* Stephen A. Harris
*Lily* Marcia Reiss
*Oak* Peter Young
*Pine* Laura Mason
*Poppy* Andrew Lack
*Snowdrop* Gail Harland
*Weeds* Nina Edwards
*Willow* Alison Syme
*Yew* Fred Hageneder

# POPPY

*Andrew Lack*

REAKTION BOOKS

*Published by*
REAKTION BOOKS LTD
Unit 32, Waterside
44–48 Wharf Road
London N1 7UX, UK

www.reaktionbooks.co.uk

First published 2016

Printed and bound in China by 1010 Printing International Ltd

A catalogue record for this book is available from the British Library

ISBN 978 1 78023 653 7

# Contents

A poppy field at Roundway Down, Wiltshire, July 2012.

# one

# What is a Poppy?

> While summer roses all their glory yield
> To crown the votary of Love and joy,
> Misfortune's victim hails, with many a sigh,
> Thee, scarlet Poppy of the pathless field,
> Gaudy, yet wild and lone; no leaf to shield
> Thy flaccid vest that, as the gale blows high,
> Flaps, and alternate folds around thy head.
> So stands in the long grass a love-crazed maid
> Smiling aghast; while stream to every wind
> Her garish ribbons, smeared with dust and rain;
> But brain-sick visions cheat her tortured mind,
> And bring false peace. Thus, lulling grief and pain,
> Kind dreams oblivious from thy juice proceed,
> Thou flimsy, showy, melancholy weed.
>
> ANNA SEWARD (1742–1809), 'To the Poppy'

The poppy: the name alone evokes thoughts that may be long forgotten or buried in memory. This must be one of the best known of all our wild flowers – beautiful, utterly distinctive and probably the first plant we consider when we think of farmland weeds. It is, in many ways, the classic weed of cornfields. It grows only on agricultural land and other cultivated or disturbed land. As a quick-growing plant with such a distinctive colour, it is bound to be noticed and almost everyone recognizes it. It can come up in such abundance that it can cover an entire cornfield with the most brilliant scarlet colour, visible from several miles away. Such fields of poppies are part of our heritage and have had a profound effect on painters, poets and other writers. On the other hand farmers may have good reason to rue the poppy's existence in their fields for all its spectacular beauty, as it can ruin crops. It has been one of our best-loved and, to farmers, most exasperating flowers ever since agriculture began in Europe. Poppies are written into European culture as deeply as any plant.

## The Meanings of Poppies

As a symbol, the poppy has meant several different things. Initially it was a symbol of fertility and new life springing from the earth, but, equally often, as in Anna Seward's sonnet, it was seen as a symbol of misfortune and a serious agricultural weed. Nowadays as a symbol it is best known for commemorating those who have died during wartime, on 'Poppy Day'.

It has found its way into several other aspects of our lives. All sorts of ornaments, from prints on dresses to brooches, earrings, trademarks and logos for various companies, are decorated with

A poppy earring, made by Rima Butkute, in its natural habitat.

Ornamental lampshade in the shape of a poppy flower, Shropshire.

poppies, especially if associated with war. Lampshades and doorknobs are made in the shape of poppy flowers. There are other associations, such as the idea of the clever person standing out as the 'tall poppy', and the Norfolk railway known as the 'Poppy Line'. There has been an increasing advent of flower names for girls. Poppy is prominent among these but there are several others, such as Lily, Rose, Daisy and Jasmine. These and others are part of the nostalgia for our relationship with the natural world that has been so eroded. The corn poppy was voted as the county flower for both Norfolk and Essex after the conservation charity Plantlife launched the idea of a floral emblem for each county in 2002.

For many people the poppy has another, and completely different, association. The poppy is the source of opium, one of the oldest and most famous of narcotics. One of the characteristics of all poppies is the production of latex, usually white or colourless, but sometimes coloured. Many members of the family are poisonous and, as with many poisonous plants, the poison can, if used carefully, be very helpful medically and/or can be a drug that leads to intoxication. The properties of opium have been known about since before

Elizabeth Blackwell's illustration of a corn poppy in *A Curious Herbal* (1737).

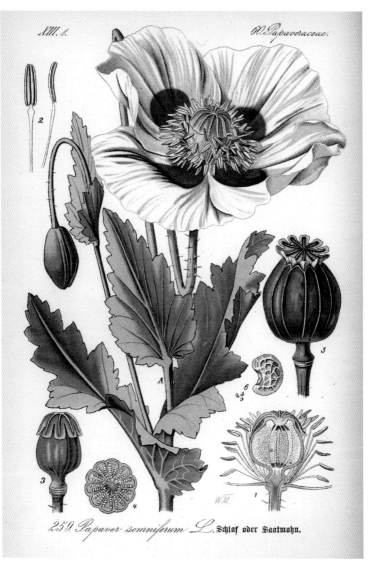

Illustration of an opium poppy from O. W. Thome,
*Flora von Deutschland, Österreich und der Schweiz* (1885).

4500 BC, and the association of poppies with drug-induced sleep or hallucination is firmly fixed in our minds.[1] A species of poppy completely different to the corn poppy provides us with these intoxicating substances, and that its flowers are normally not red at all but a dull white or violet (it does have a red form but this is less common) does not affect the association – it is still a poppy. The two species are frequently mixed up in folklore, literature and the public imagination, and 'the poppy' has often been described both as a scarlet agricultural weed and as possessing narcotic properties. The opium poppy has the greatest concentration of such substances and the widest uses. The corn poppy contains small quantities of rhoeadine, which does have mild sedative qualities and has been used in pain relief or insomnia, but comes nowhere near opium in effectiveness.

This book is about both the corn poppy and the opium poppy, different though they are, and other members of this beautiful family. We will look at all the associations and their implications in this book, as well as the equally fascinating biology of these remarkable plants.

## The Names

The poppy has been a familiar plant since antiquity, and the derivation of its names beyond the ancient roots of European languages are obscure, but the word poppy, and the names for the plant in many European languages, *pavot* in French, *pipacs* in Hungarian, *paparoúna* in modern Greek and others, derive from the Latin name for the plant, *papaver*. This word may itself stem from the earliest agriculture in ancient Mesopotamia, around 4000 BC. An Assyrian document, as far as we can tell, refers to the poppy juice as *pa pa*.[2] The word may otherwise come from the Latin *pappa*, meaning soft food or baby food, and *ferre* (to bear), because of the latex – often milky – that oozes from the stems of all poppies. Whatever its origin, the Latin word *papaver* is used as the scientific name for the main genus of European poppies today.

| | |
|---|---|
| Blind Eyes | (Northants) |
| Blind Man | (Wilts.) |
| Blindy Buffs | (Yorks.) |
| Bull's Eyes | (Somerset) |
| Butterfly Ladies | (Somerset) |
| Canker; Canker-rose | (East Anglia) |
| Cheesebowls | (Somerset) |
| Cockeno | (Northumb.) |
| Cock-rose; Cock's-comb; Cock's Head | (Yorks., Scotland) |
| Collinhood | (Roxburgh, Lothian) |
| Cop-rose; Cup-rose | (various) |
| Cornflower; Corn-rose | (Devon, Dorset, Somerset) |
| Cusk | (Warwicks.) |
| Devil's Tongue | (Cornwall) |
| Earaches | (Derbys., Notts.) |
| Fireflout | (Somerset, Northumb.) |
| Gollywogs | (Somerset) |
| Gye | (Suffolk) |
| Headache | (various) |
| Hogweed | (East Anglia) |
| Lightnings | (Northumb.) |
| Old Woman's Petticoat | (Somerset) |
| Paradise Lily | (Somerset) |
| Pepper Boxes | (Somerset) |
| Poison Poppy; Poppet; Popple | (various) |
| Redcap; Redcup; Red Dolly; Red Huntsman; Red Nap; Red Soldiers | (all Somerset) |
| Red Petticoat | (Kent) |
| Red Rags | (Dorset) |
| Red-weed | (various) |
| Sleepyhead | (Somerset) |
| Soldiers | (various) |
| Thunderball | (Warwicks.) |
| Thunderbolt | (various) |
| Thundercup; Thunderflower | (Wilts., Berwicks.) |
| Wartflower | (Cornwall) |
| Wild Maws | (Derbys.) |

Names for the corn (common) poppy, and their county of origin, as noted in Geoffrey Grigson, *The Englishman's Flora* (1955).[3]

The ancient Greek name was *mekon*. This may have its origins in the myth of Prometheus who famously stole fire back from Zeus after the god had hidden it from humans at Mekone. It is possible that actually this is the other way round: the place being named after the poppy, because it was a common feature of the landscape there. The poppy is, unsurprisingly, associated with fire because of its colour. The Greek name has been given to the genus, *Meconopsis*, and we use the word 'meconium' to describe the faecal discharge from a new-born because of its resemblance to the juice of a poppy. The Slavic name for the poppy is *mak* and is probably from the same root. In German, Dutch and Scandinavian languages the name for the plant is *mohn* or *vallmo* or some variant, deriving from the Old Norse name, possibly connected with the Greek. The word 'opium' derives from the Greek *opos*, meaning plant sap.

As we might expect with such a well-known plant, there have been many other countrypeople's names for the poppy. Geoffrey Grigson compiled a list for his *Englishman's Flora* of 1955.[4] Many of these names come from the West Country, perhaps because he was based first in Cornwall and then Wiltshire. Some of the names illus-trate the folklore of the plant that will be discussed in this book. In French too, one alternative name is the *coquelicot* used most famously by Claude Monet in his paintings of poppies. This literally means a cock crow, like some English country names, because of the similar colour of the cockscomb.

## The Origin of Poppies

The story of the poppy has to begin where poppies began. And we immediately find our first difficulty: where do poppies come from? The familiar corn, or common, poppy, *Papaver rhoeas*, is distributed across the whole of temperate Europe, much of temperate Asia, North Africa and large areas in North America. We know that it was introduced, probably accidentally with crop plants, into North America by Europeans, but what about the rest of its range? Poppies

Kitagawa Sosetsu,
*Poppies*, 1640s,
hanging scroll.

grow in cornfields, on roadsides and in other disturbed places but, in northern Europe at least, only in such habitats. These did not exist in Britain or the rest of northern Europe before about 7,000 years ago when agriculture first spread from the Middle East. The first definite evidence of corn poppies in Britain comes from Neolithic excavations dating from 3500 to 2500 BC.[5]

Agriculture originally appeared around 12,000 years ago in the Fertile Crescent of mountains running through Syria, southern Turkey and northern Iraq. It was the largest single change in human lifestyles that has ever occurred. Before this change, there had been some manipulation of the environment with the use of fire and encouragement of certain plants, but agriculture took this to a whole new level of management and led to man becoming fixed to a territory which was then his own. Agriculture spread into ancient Mesopotamia, in what is now Iraq, and this led to the first settled towns and cities and the first instances of writing. This practice spread in all directions, including into southeastern Europe, and then gradually north and west with farming techniques gradually becoming more sophisticated. Farmers brought with them their domestic animals – mainly sheep and goats – crops such as wheat and barley and, following these and intimately associated with them, those plants that we have come to call weeds. The poppy must have been among these, suggesting that its status within Britain is not actually that of a 'native' plant, in the sense of arriving in the British Isles without any help from human migration.

It is possible that the poppy was introduced deliberately, but it is likely that the human help was inadvertent; the poppy and other weeds could simply thrive in the agricultural environment that we provided for them. Those plants that spread in early civilizations have become known as 'archaeophytes'.[6] These are defined as plants introduced by humans at some point before AD 1500, but many archaeophytes are cornfield weeds, like the poppy. These were probably introduced by accident at some point since agriculture started, but, regardless, long before 1500. What is clear is that the poppy and other weeds spread extremely successfully, and became thoroughly established as weeds of cereal crops.

To work out where the corn poppy is likely to have appeared originally as a species, we need to look at its closest relatives and see where these species live today. The agricultural habitat has only existed for about 12,000 years, which is not particularly long in the lifetime of a plant species. Many species will not have changed at all in that time, and those that have will retain numerous features that are similar to what they would have been 12,000 years ago.

Semitic poppy, *Papaver umbonatum*, a close relative of the corn poppy, native to Israel, Palestine, Lebanon and Syria.

There are about 32 species in the genus *Papaver*, and the centre of distribution of the genus is in southwest Asia and the eastern Mediterranean. Those species that are most closely related to the corn poppy are clustered here, especially in the Holy Land, and adjacent parts of the Middle East and southwest Asia. There appear to be up to seven species that are closely related to the corn poppy. Three in particular, native to the eastern Mediterranean, are very similar.[7] These are the 'Semitic Poppy', *Papaver umbonatum*, the 'Humble Poppy', *Papaver humile*, and the 'Carmel Poppy', *Papaver carmeli*. These three species can all hybridize with the corn poppy and can be referred to as the 'corn poppy' in general terms as they are so similar in appearance. The hybrids are fertile, showing that these species are indeed very closely related. In the past, some authors have considered them as variants of one species.

The only one of these species to have spread out of this area is the corn poppy and, even within the area, it is the species most characteristic of the agricultural fields. The three related red poppy species occur in disturbed places in the eastern Mediterranean, sometimes in open parts of shrubland ('garrigue') or on coasts. They can occur in ploughed land, but are not so markedly associated with agricultural fields as the corn poppy. There is an intriguing possibility that the corn poppy, as we define it today, is a species that only appeared with the advent of agriculture. If this is right, the species has only existed in its current form for less than 12,000 years and arose as a hybrid between two of these closest relatives, or possibly as a result of multiple hybridizations between all three.[8]

Hybrids between closely related species, when they are viable at all, can be particularly strong and vigorous, with the combination of genes from more than one parental species. But they are frequently sterile; the reproductive cells fail to form because the chromosomes are too dissimilar to form exact pairs needed in the production of the reproductive cells. The most obvious example is the mule, famously tough and resilient but almost always sterile. Perhaps horse and donkey are too distant to allow for the sperm and eggs to form. In plants, hybrids are often partially sterile but not fully. If they can produce pollen or ovules then, given a few generations, reproductive problems can disappear, with fertile forms surviving well. We do not know whether this happened with our corn poppy but it seems entirely possible. If so, and the hybrids gained extra vigour, this could be one reason why it has spread so successfully. A parallel situation that is well documented is found in the Oxford ragwort, *Senecio squalidus*. This was introduced to Oxford from Mount Etna in Sicily in the seventeenth century. It has been shown to be a hybrid between two Sicilian species that has stabilized in Britain to a distinct form, and has spread widely around the country along railways, building sites and other derelict places.[9]

If the corn poppy is native to the eastern Mediterranean it has, clearly, been able to adapt to a very different climate in order to spread across the rest of Europe. Those parts of the eastern Mediterranean where it probably originated have hot dry summers and cool, wetter winters with rather unpredictable rainfall. These conditions are particularly suited to short-lived plants that grow rapidly when conditions are good in the winter and set abundant seeds, but die off for the summer drought when growth is difficult. Many plants survive purely as seeds over the dry summer, when the lack of plant cover can lead to unstable soils. Many of our staple seed crop plants grow like that, especially wheat and barley. They are suitable as crop plants partly because they are short-lived and put many of their resources into seeds. Perhaps it is not surprising that agriculture started in this region.

There are many agricultural weeds that are confined to the Mediterranean region and only some species that have been able to adapt to the more northerly climate and become more widespread. Further north and west in Europe the summer will be the growing season and the winter the dormant season, but agriculture provides a similarly disturbed habitat, with soil constantly being ploughed and left bare immediately before a growing season. It seems that several of those species that could adapt became very successful following the plough across Europe. Many of these, including the poppy, have seeds that can lie dormant not just over the winter months but for many years. This too can be a vital characteristic in the agricultural environment when some seasons or crops may not provide ideal conditions for growth.

The corn poppy, from the evidence, almost certainly arose in the eastern Mediterranean. In some parts of Europe, especially in eastern Europe, but also in France and other countries, we can still see the magnificent swathes of red that excite strong emotions and have so captivated artists and poets over the centuries.

## British Poppies

In Britain there are actually four species of red poppies growing wild, all of them annuals of cultivated and disturbed land. They are all associated almost entirely with agriculture. The corn poppy is by far the commonest species across England, Wales and much of lowland Scotland. It is the only one that can colour an entire field and, if I refer simply to the 'poppy' in this book, this is the species I mean. It is usually a bright scarlet colour but this colour does vary a little. I have seen colours ranging from a distinct orangey-red through to a deep red colour within the same field.

The three other species are less familiar. These are all quite similar to each other, though each has a different shade of red and some

Long-headed poppy. *Papaver dubium.*

Prickly poppy. *Papaver argemone* and a rough poppy. *Papaver hybridum.*

other distinguishing features. The long-headed poppy, *Papaver dubium*, is the other fairly common species. This has a slightly smaller flower with a paler, more pinkish colour, but can be overlooked because of its similarity to the corn poppy. Its 'long head' is the elongated seed-pod, different in shape from the rounded pod of the corn poppy. It occurs fairly commonly on roadsides, field margins and waste ground and extends further north and west in Scotland than the corn poppy. The prickly poppy, *Papaver argemone*, has a much smaller and paler flower than the corn poppy. It occurs rather sparsely across much of central and southeast England and with outlying populations elsewhere. It is found on well-drained sandy, chalky or limestone soils. The rough poppy, *Papaver hybridum*, is the rarest of the four and confined to field margins on the chalk of southeast England. It has small flowers with a rich deep crimson colour. The seed-pods of both the rough and prickly poppies are covered with bristles, unlike the smooth capsules of the two commoner species.

The long-headed, prickly and rough poppies come from different sections of the genus from the corn poppy so are not its closest relatives, but they all originate from further south in Europe as well. The commonest of them, the long-headed *P. dubium*, appears to have come from Austria or Slovakia and the other two from the eastern Mediterranean, like the corn poppy.[10]

Welsh poppy, *Papaver (Meconopsis) cambricum*, showing nodding bud typical of poppies and sepals at petal tip on the opening bud. Garden at Cynwyl Elfed, Carmarthenshire.

There are differences in chromosome numbers among the poppies. Among plants, changes in chromosome number are common. A diploid plant (or animal) is one with what we think of as the standard two sets of chromosomes, one set from each parent. An individual with four sets of chromosomes may arise spontaneously by a doubling of this number of chromosomes from a failure of cell division at some point in the reproductive cycle. This is quite common in plants, and the resultant plants are known as tetraploids. Four chromosome sets can also appear after a hybridization between two species has led to partial sterility. The original hybrid will have the normal diploid number, but if the number of chromosomes then doubles, the plant may be able to produce fertile reproductive cells and becomes tetraploid. It is likely to be fertile only with other tetraploids and not with its parental species so, in effect, it becomes a new species in a single generation. We do not know how often this has happened among the poppies. The corn poppy is diploid, along with its closest relatives in the eastern Mediterranean, and the rough poppy, with a chromosome number of $2n=14$. The long-headed is usually tetraploid with 28 chromosomes but can have 42, perhaps a result of multiple hybridizations somewhere in its ancestry. The prickly poppy also has 42.

Two other members of the poppy family occur naturally in Britain, both with yellow flowers. The beautiful Welsh poppy, *Papaver* (*Meconopsis*) *cambricum*, is native to damp rock ledges and upland woods in Wales, Ireland and Devon and possibly elsewhere. It is popular as a garden plant too and has spread widely from gardens into hedge banks and roadsides, becoming naturalized across most of the country. The yellow horned poppy, *Glaucium flavum*, is a striking plant with extremely glaucous (blue-green) stems and leaves, and enormously long fruits, the 'horns' of its name. It grows on shingle beaches, and occasionally sand dunes or sea cliffs, mainly in the south and east but as far north as southern Scotland.

One other yellow-flowered species in the family, the greater celandine, *Chelidonium majus*, is not so obviously a poppy, with its much smaller flowers, but has many features typical of poppies. It is widely distributed in Europe, especially as a garden and wayside weed, but

Yellow horned poppy, *Glaucium flavum*, Thorpeness, Suffolk.

Greater celandine, *Chelidonium majus*, cut stem with latex.

appears to have been introduced into Britain. It has latex of a brilliant orange that has long been used as an analgesic, a treatment for warts and skin problems, cauterizing wounds and other ailments. It was probably introduced for its medicinal properties as a potherb in Roman times, like several other archaeophytes. 'Greater celandine' is an unexpected name as it has no direct botanical connection with the well-known lesser celandine, a common member of the buttercup family. 'Celandine', and the Latin name of the greater celandine, *Chelidonium*, are derived from the Greek word for a swallow, *Chelidon*, and it derives from the curious belief that swallows put the latex of the greater celandine onto the eyes of their young to restore their sight.[11] The lesser celandine, *Ficaria verna*, has no such folklore attached to it, but it flowers early in the year so the connection with swallows is presumably that both are harbingers of spring.

Several other species can spread themselves within gardens and a few are naturalized, usually in waste places and on roadsides, the most common being the opium poppy, *Papaver somniferum*, the California poppy, *Eschscholzia californica*, and the oriental poppy, *Papaver orientale*.

In Europe as a whole, there are around nineteen species of native poppy. These and the other poppies of the world and the related fumitories are now placed in the same family.

Greater celandine, growing as a naturalized weed in the Czech Republic.

Lesser celandine.

*Hypecoum procumbens*, a plant with intermediate characters
between poppies and fumitories.

## two

# The Poppy Family

**T**he poppy family, the Papaveraceae, has been considered as a natural family of 200–250 species, including all the species we would regard as poppies and a few others that are clearly related to them such as the greater celandine and the bloodroot. It has long been recognized that the family shares a number of characteristics with another family, the Fumariaceae, which consists of around 570 herbaceous species including the fumitories, which are weeds of farmland and hedgerow, and corydalis and bleeding hearts, which are well-known garden plants. I will refer to them collectively as the fumitories. These have very different-looking, and usually much smaller, flowers in inflorescences. Despite these differences they have been regarded as sister families, and two of the lesser-known genera, *Hypecoum*, about fifteen species of 'little poppies', and the fern poppy, *Pteridophyllum racemosum*, are somewhat intermediate in character between the two families. Now we have a study of the DNA and other molecular characters and this has fully confirmed that the two families are indeed very closely related.[1] So much so that, in the most modern classification, they have been amalgamated into one larger family, still known as the Papaveraceae. The two former families are now the main subfamilies Papaveroideae and Fumarioideae. The family is classified in the major group, eudicotyledons, which includes nearly 70 per cent of all flowering plants. This enlarged poppy family is related to buttercups in the basal lineage of the eudicotyledons.

The majority of poppies are herbaceous annuals or perennials. There are a few shrubs: two species of magnificent white-flowered tree poppies of California in the genus *Romneya*, another two species (sometimes split into more) of yellow-flowered tree poppies, *Dendromecon*, again from California, one shrubby prickly poppy, *Argemone fruticosa*, from Mexico and nine species of tropical and little-known 'tree celandines', *Bocconia*.[2] The leaves of the great majority of poppies are much divided into segments and many are slightly glaucous – with a bluish tinge like those of the opium poppy. A few have undivided leaves.

One characteristic feature of the poppy subfamily is the presence of latex that oozes from cut stems and leaves.[3] This is most commonly white or colourless, but it can be yellow, orange or even a rich orangey-red in the well-named eastern North American plant the bloodroot, *Sanguinaria canadensis*. Most plants have what are collectively known as secondary compounds – those not directly involved in the structure or functioning of the plant. These are usually seen as the plant's defences, as many are at least mildly poisonous to insects or inhibit digestion. Tannins, such as those found in tea,

Common fumitory, a cornfield weed related to the poppies, Yorkshire.

are a well-known example. Some are known as alkaloids, and a range of alkaloid substances have been recorded in poppies and in the fumitories, although the opium poppy has the greatest concentration. Many of these substances are at least mildly poisonous, and some are narcotic. In poppies they are concentrated in the latex. Ancient herbal uses and modern medicinal uses are found in many species of poppy, not just the opium poppy.

The flowers of the whole Papaveroideae subfamily are rather unusual in form.[4] In most species, including the best-known poppies, the numbers of floral parts are based on the number two. The flower has an outermost whorl of two sepals, which protect the developing bud, but, in nearly all species, these drop off as the flower opens. Inside the sepals there are two whorls of two petals each, so four in all, but two clearly inside the other two. There are numerous stamens forming a striking boss, often of a different colour from the rest of the flower. Inside this there may be just two ovaries or a multiple of two, or many in most poppies. These fuse together to form the fruit capsule containing numerous small seeds.

Some white- or yellow-flowered poppies in the New World, part of a distinct section within the subfamily, have parts in threes, with three sepals and six petals in two whorls of three. These include some species of prickly poppies in the genus *Argemone*, the tree *Romneya* species and the few species of small-flowered western North American *Platystemon*, *Platystigma* and *Meconella*. Finally the bloodroot has eight petals in two whorls of four, but only two sepals. All the flowers except *Hypecoum* and *Pteridophyllum* are, at least nearly, radially symmetrical – the petals are alike and the flower has more than one plane of symmetry. Cultivated forms, and the occasional wild individual of any species, may have other numbers of petals.

The flowers can be almost any colour. The bright scarlet and other shades of red so typical of our best-known poppies are just one form. There are pinks and yellows, oranges, purples, pristine white and the luscious blues of the large Himalayan poppies. Cultivated forms of the well-known garden species range widely in colour too.

The stems bearing the capsules are flexible in many species and the seeds are mainly shed through pores as in the corn poppy.

The fumitories characteristically have four petals like the poppies, but in these plants the four petals do not all look alike. Often the outer two petals differ from the inner two and, in some, the two outer petals are themselves different shapes. The flowers in most species face outwards with a bilateral symmetry – that is, only one vertical plane of symmetry. Many create a tubular, lipped form quite unlike the poppies' four regular petals and, superficially, more

Bleeding heart. *Dicentra spectabilis.*

resembling the flowers of a snapdragon or dead-nettle. In the bleeding hearts the flowers hang downwards. Most species of fumitory have only four stamens, unlike the boss of many stamens present in the poppies.

Four-petalled flowers, like those of most poppies, are found in only a few other families, especially the cabbage family, the willow-herb family, the European bedstraws (though not the tropical members of this large family), a few members of the rose family and the

Paul de Longpré, *Poppies and Bees*, 1906, watercolour. An opium poppy depicted with six petals instead of the normal four.

occasional other species. None of these is particularly close to the poppies. The commonest number of floral parts in eudicotyledons is five, as in roses, buttercups and many others. The possession of six petals, as in some yellow or white New World poppies, is even more unusual. These plants have three sepals and, as with the four-petalled flowers, two whorls of petals, here each whorl with three. Floral parts in threes are characteristic of the other major group of flowering plants, the monocotyledons, which includes the orchids and the majority of bulbous plants, but these all have a single whorl of three petals. Their flowers can resemble those of the six-petalled poppies in symmetry since many lilies, daffodils and some other monocotyledons have petals and sepals that look alike, making them appear to have six petals.

The occasional plant of many species of poppy can be found with other numbers of petals, and even sometimes just one flower on an otherwise normal plant has five or another number as a developmental abnormality. In cultivation this is more frequent.

## The Distribution of Poppies

Members of the poppy (sub)family are naturally found mainly in the temperate regions of the northern hemisphere. Species extend right the way across from western North America to Japan. Several species occur in the subtropical and tropical regions of Mexico and Central America and a few in South America, mainly in the Andes. There are several in subtropical southern Asia, including the great blue Himalayan poppies, and one poppy is native to southern Africa. Various poppies have been introduced outside their native range and you can find a poppy now in most parts of the temperate and subtropical world. The fumitory subfamily is also mainly north temperate extending to southern Africa.

Rather surprisingly for what seems such a delicate plant, there are two poppy species in the Arctic and several more near the snow-line on mountains. Most plants in these extreme conditions with a

Arctic poppy, *Papaver radicatum*, with dwarf willow, Norway.

very short growing season form a cushion of leaves with short flower heads, but the pale yellow Arctic poppy, *Papaver radicatum*, though small for a poppy, has the typical poppy form of divided leaves and a flexible flowering stem. It occurs quite commonly right around the Arctic region and, in fact, has the distinction of being one of the most cold-hardy flowering plants in the world, along with the Arctic mouse-ear and the purple saxifrage, occurring on mountains in Greenland at an altitude of 970 m (3,180 ft) in Pearyland at latitude 83° north.[5]

## Ornamental Plants

Poppies are so showy, so variable in colour and many are so easy to grow that they have been popular garden plants for centuries. There are annual plants, some herbaceous perennials, and the shrubby 'tree poppies', all popular in gardens. Cultivated forms of several species quite frequently find their way onto waste ground or other disturbed sites within Britain and elsewhere, especially varieties of corn poppy, opium poppy, oriental poppy and California poppy.

Ted Hughes celebrated garden poppies with his poem 'Big Poppy' that begins: 'Hot-eyed Mafia Queen! At the trim garden's edge / She sways towards August'. Hughes's poppy drugs the bumblebees or visiting flies, but flings its 'royal carpet' of petals away as it quickly withers.

## Varieties of Corn and Opium Poppy

The annuals need to grow from seed each year, but the most popular annuals usually do this prolifically and a gardener is as likely to be pulling up what he does not want as carefully nurturing new seedlings. The corn poppy provides us handsomely with good garden annuals. It has been bred extensively to produce many different colour forms. Among the best known of these are the 'Shirley' poppies. These are among the most frequently sold of all poppies, usually as a packet of seeds. They can be a delight to plant as they come in a variety of reds, pinks, whites and variegated forms and you never know what is going to come up, though nearly always several different colours will be mixed in.

The Shirley poppies all started with the Revd William Wilks, vicar of the Surrey village of Shirley and a keen horticulturist. In 1879 or thereabouts he found a single corn poppy in a wild corner of his garden that had a flower with a white fringe around the red. Intrigued by this and what might come of it, he investigated further and collected the seeds. Around 200 poppies grew up and, of these, five had flowers with the white fringe. He had begun a selective breeding programme and evidently became hooked on the project.[6] He was interested to see what colours and forms might eventually appear, and whether he could breed out the central black spot in the petals. After many generations of selective breeding he managed to produce pure white poppies and every intermediate between white and red, with varying and unpredictable amounts of borders, spotting or

'Shirley' poppy, a descendant of Wilks's breeding programme, with white centre, Oxfordshire.

A semi-double Shirley poppy, with a hoverfly, Oxford.

speckling with white, and with mainly white or yellow centres. Wilks became the Royal Horticultural Society's longest-serving secretary (1888–1920) and was eventually awarded the Royal Horticultural Society's highest honour, its Victoria medal, in 1912. The wrought iron gate to its garden at Wisley, erected in 1926, three years after his death, is known as the Wilks gate and bears a poppy emblem.

Among the poppies that Wilks bred appeared some with 'double' flowers. Wilks did not regard these as 'true' Shirley poppies. True Shirleys were single with a white base and pale stamens.[7] In double flowers, nothing is actually doubled. Usually one or more whorls of stamens become petals. If just one or two whorls have become petals the flower is sometimes known as 'semi-double', a phrase that, if taken literally, would surely bring us back to single! Fully 'double' flowers have more of the stamens becoming petals. Roses and carnations are the best-known double flowers. Often, even in double flowers, a few stamens remain and the plants can retain some pollen and thus some male fertility. The carpels are unaffected, so they will remain capable of producing seeds. Double flowers can have a large and indefinite number of petals.

Double poppy showing that all stamens have become petals.
Probably descended from the Shirley poppies.

Johanna Helena Graff, *A Poppy in Three Stages of Flowering, with a Caterpillar, Pupa and Butterfly*, late 17th–early 18th century, watercolour.
This shows a double form of the opium poppy.

Shirley is now part of Croydon, in effect a suburb of south London, and the name survives as a park, mainly laid out as a golf course and sports facilities. At least until the 1980s, variegated poppies would occasionally turn up. Poppies have long-lived seeds, so there is always a chance of turning one up that has been long buried. A pub was built when Shirley became a housing estate around 1935, and was named The Shirley Poppy after its most famous flower. Unfortunately the picture on the pub sign was a black-centred scarlet corn poppy, the ancestor of course, but not one of Wilks's Shirleys! Sadly, like so many pubs around the country, it went out of business, and it is now a McDonald's restaurant. In 2009 in honour of Revd Wilks the church in Shirley planted some Shirley poppies in the churchyard and, to their delight, one came up on Wilks's grave and flowered in 2010.

The opium poppy is grown in gardens for its floral display, and it too has many different colour varieties that can make an attractive show. The most popular are usually sold as 'peony-flowered' varieties, double flowers often with frilly petals and with a great variety of colours. Unlike the corn poppy, these have a rather heady fragrance. The seeds can be collected for culinary use.

## California Poppy

The California poppy, *Eschscholzia californica*, is, in addition to the corn poppy, the one that has given rise to the most eulogies about its colour. It has the most strikingly lustrous yellowy-orange colour and the novelist John Steinbeck gives it this poetic description: 'of a burning colour, not orange, not gold, but if pure gold were liquid and could raise a cream, that golden cream might be like the color of poppies'.[8] This plant has produced an outpouring of purple prose, perhaps exemplified best by an offering from the *Pittsburgh Press* on 2 May 1902:

> Far out at sea glimmering sheets of dazzling gold arrested
> the gaze of the early explorers of California. . . . Dream-like

in beauty, fascinated from sheer loveliness spreading
its soft undulations over the land, the California
poppy bloomed above the richest veins and arteries
of gold the world has ever known, all unsuspected.
A Circe, with powers to please, dazzle and charm by
its enchantments, while it allures, lulls and mystifies,
this flower of sleep seemed to draw by some occult process
from the earth the elixir of gold, unfolding its blossoms
of gold as beacons proclaiming: 'We are blooming above
rich mines of gold.'[9]

California's 'gold rush' of 1848—55 had by then become legendary but, by deliberately mixing up the flowers with the presence of actual gold, this article demonstrates that California has two reasons to be called the 'Golden State'. Any mention of a poppy, it seems, has to include a reference to sleep-making properties, and opium was popular and well known in America by the time this was written (see Chapter Seven). As with most poppies, there is a very slight narcotic effect with the California poppy, and various tinctures of California poppy are sold with this in mind.[10] Some people evidently find it a useful sleeping draught, but the effect, perhaps fortunately, is very small.

The California poppy derives its almost unpronounceable genus name from Dr J. F. von Eschscholtz, a surgeon and naturalist on Russian expeditions to North America's west coast in 1816 and 1824. The poppy's name is best pronounced 'esholtsia'. It is normally bright yellowy-orange, but varies considerably in the wild between this and white and, in cultivation, extends to red forms and a whole range of intermediates. It can be perennial in its native range but it is best treated as an annual in Britain. It is normally very easy to grow if it has a good, sunny, well-drained soil. Though short-lived, it often seeds itself vigorously in a spot it likes.

It is the state flower of California. In California the local Native Americans used the seeds for food before European colonization. It has been introduced into other parts of the world with a

California poppy, *Eschscholzia californica*.

Mediterranean climate and has naturalized in many places, usually on bare or waste ground. Emory Smith wrote a book about it in 1902.[11]

There are actually about nine other species of *Eschscholzia*, all yellow- or orange-flowered with occasional white forms, and all from western North America, but *E. californica* is the only one found commonly in cultivation.[12] The Mexican tulip poppy, *Hunnemannia fumariifolia*, is similar and has particularly large flowers, but is a bit tender in British gardens. It is perennial in its native land, but if sown as an annual, it can make a striking display.

## Some Perennial Poppies

One of the most popular garden poppies is the perennial 'oriental' poppy. This is usually sold as *Papaver orientalis* (or, more correctly, *P. orientale*) but the cultivated varieties actually derive from hybrids between the wild *Papaver orientale* and the larger *P. bracteatum* and, perhaps, a third species, *P. pseudo-orientale*, that may itself be of hybrid origin between the other two. All of these come originally from the Caucasus and northeastern Turkey. They come in many sizes and colours and there are several double cultivars, some with a huge number of petals. They make excellent, robust garden border plants, flowering in the early summer. They are easy to grow as long as the soil is not too wet.

On rock gardens the perennial alpine and Iceland poppies are often grown. These are usually sold as *Papaver alpinum* and *P. nudicaule* respectively, though both names are ambiguous. These plants undoubtedly derive from hybrids of several other species, the alpine poppy apparently from at least five species, including the white

Oriental poppy flowering in an abandoned garden, Goring, Oxfordshire.

Oriental poppy
by Jean-Nicolas de
La Hire, from his
four-volume series
of botanical drawings
and transfer prints
made in Paris,
c. 1720.

*Papaver Orientale hirsutissimum, Flore magno Carduus*
*Pavot d'Orient tres-velu, a grande fleur.*

*P. burseri*, as well as several yellow or reddish species; the Iceland
poppy from at least four.[13] They make a wide range of reds through
yellows to white in a garden and, though short-lived, often seed
themselves. They hybridize readily.

One native British perennial poppy, the yellow-flowered Welsh
poppy, is often grown in gardens. This was named *Papaver cambricum*
by Linnaeus in the eighteenth century, but was renamed *Meconopsis
cambrica* in 1814 as the type species of the new genus. It makes an
excellent garden plant, being easy to grow, and it has escaped quite
widely from gardens, planting itself in many places across the country.

Explorers in the late nineteenth century collected some other
plants that they placed in the Welsh poppy genus, *Meconopsis*. These
are the glorious blue poppies from the Himalayas. Stories of these

plants were, at first, widely disbelieved – who had ever heard of a blue poppy? But seeds were brought back to Britain and, once they flowered, they aroused intense interest as garden plants. The first to arrive was the elegant M. *wallichii* in the 1850s but this was outshone particularly by two large and intensely blue species, M. *grandis* around the turn of the century and M. *betonicifolia* in the 1920s. When grown in drifts in a large garden, the effect is magnificent. Others have been introduced since.[14] They are among our finest garden plants of any kind and are always treasured and admired wherever they grow successfully. They have a reputation for being difficult to grow but this reputation largely comes from those living in the densely populated warmer and drier regions of Britain. In their native Himalayas these poppies experience cold winters and wet summers. Perhaps it is not surprising that they thrive especially in our northern gardens on acid soils where the conditions most closely resemble those in

Himalayan poppy, *Meconopsis betonicifolia*.

Himalayan blue poppy, *Meconopsis aculeata*, in its native Kullu valley, west Himalayas.

their native land. In these places, give them a deep rich moist soil that does not dry out in the summer and they should thrive.

There are now altogether more than forty species of *Meconopsis* described, mostly perennials, although some are monocarpic; that is, they may live for one or more years as leaf rosettes before flowering once and then dying. Several have come into cultivation.

There is one peculiarity of the naming of *Meconopsis* that has arisen. It was coined for the fact that, where *Papaver* has a stigmatic disc above the ovary, the Welsh poppy has a short style and no disc. The Himalayan blue poppies are like the Welsh poppy in this respect and so are included in the genus. But, as knowledge of the genus

Joseph-Pierre Buch'oz, 'Horned Poppy', in *Collection précieuse et enluminée des fleurs les plus belles et les plus curieuses* . . . (1776).

increased, it became increasingly clear that the Welsh poppy was rather unlike the Asian species. Firstly, it is completely isolated, with a western European distribution, whereas all the others are Asian. Secondly it has a few features of seeds and pollen that are unlike the Asian members of the genus and more like those of *Papaver*. In addition, only two other *Meconopsis* species have yellow flowers and they look rather different. With DNA testing it has now been shown that our Welsh poppy is more closely related to the corn poppy than to the other *Meconopsis* species found in Asia.[15] It should be known as *Papaver cambricum*, its original name. This immediately throws the whole genus name into doubt, as the Welsh poppy was the original species, the 'type' of the genus. Taxonomists are notorious sticklers for protocol and, in theory, a new genus name would be needed for the Himalayan species as *Meconopsis* became invalid. Fortunately this story had a happy ending. In 2014 common sense prevailed under the little-used rule of *nomen conservandum*, invoked when a name is well known and unambiguous so can be conserved, overriding the strict rules of taxonomy. Our Welsh Poppy is *Papaver cambricum* and the Himalayan beauties retain *Meconopsis* as their genus.[16]

The yellow horned poppy, *Glaucium flavum*, and one or two others in the genus can make striking border plants with their glaucous leaves as well as yellow flowers. They need space, sun and well-drained soil. They thrive best in poor soil, unsurprisingly for a plant of shingle beaches. In a rich soil they are usually annual, but give them a gravel path or wall edge and they will live for several years and can seed themselves.

There are several other splendid garden plants among this varied family. The two species of *Romneya* tree poppies of California are especially spectacular with their satiny white flowers and massive boss of yellow stamens. They can grow to 7 m (23 ft) tall but are usually best pruned and trained to about 3 m (10 ft) against a sunny south-facing wall or other sheltered sunlit position. They are quite hardy in Britain despite their southern provenance. The yellow tree poppy, *Dendromecon rigida*, another Californian plant, can also be most

Bloodroot, *Sanguinaria canadensis*, cultivated double form.

effective against a sunny wall, although it is more tender than the *Romneya* species and grows best in the warmest parts of the country. The prickly poppy, *Argemone mexicana*, is another yellow-flowered species of larger borders.

Several other close relatives of the true poppies, all in the subfamily Papaveroideae, commonly find their way into our gardens. The most widespread of all is the greater celandine, *Chelidonium majus*, a short-lived perennial that seeds itself readily in many gardens. It has fairly modest yellow flowers for its family, but its requirements are few, and it obligingly fills shady spots, even those with poor soil. The bloodroot, *Sanguinaria canadensis*, does not really look much like a poppy but makes an excellent garden plant. It is a low-growing perennial of shady places with bright white flowers and is widely planted, usually in its double form. It can grow in great abundance in the woods of its native eastern North America and is best seen in masses. Finally a most unpoppy-like genus, *Macleaya*, native to China and Japan, gives us two species of tall perennials that grow well in shady woodland spots. They grow up to 2.5 m (8 ft) with panicles of tiny flowers and glaucous leaves and are widely planted in large formal gardens.

Tree poppy, *Romneya trichocalyx*, at Stonor Park, Oxfordshire.

Prickly poppy, *Argemone mexicana*, University Parks, Oxford.

A plumed poppy, *Macleaya cordata*, found in Stonor Park, Oxfordshire, though native to China and Japan.

There is little doubt that more species from this spectacular family could make excellent garden plants, and more are planted in a few specialist gardens. The main reason that others are not planted more widely is that there is such a variety within the few well-known species that further species are perhaps unnecessary.

# *three*
# The Colour

The colour of the poppy alone is often enough to identify it. Even a single poppy plant makes its presence obvious, and an entire field always turns heads. The poppy flower looks extremely delicate, partly because the two sepals that protect the flowers in bud drop off as the flower opens. The petals are large, but thin, often crumpled-looking and partly translucent, so the quality of the colour looks different in different lights. The bright scarlet of midday can turn to a glorious orange-red as the setting sun shines through the petals. The instant recognition comes from the fact that this is such an unusual colour in the European flora as a whole, and a particularly unusual one in the British flora. This colour is one of the major factors that have led to so much folklore and symbolic association surrounding the poppy.

Sylvia Plath was clearly upset by the colour of the poppy flowers in her poem 'Poppies in July' that starts 'Little poppies, little hell flames', and complains that it is exhausting to watch them. In her later poem, 'Poppies in October', she is more celebratory: 'Even the sun-clouds this morning cannot manage such skirts.'

In Britain there is a native flora of around 1,500 species, and other colours are well represented. There are numerous inconspicuous greenish flowers, many yellow, purple and blue flowers and a particularly large number of white flowers but, with the exception of poppies, only two are a genuine scarlet: the scarlet pimpernel and the pheasant's-eye, which are considered later.

A single poppy plant on the edge of a cornfield, Yorkshire.

Red form of the turban buttercup, *Ranunculus asiaticus*.

We have seen that poppies almost certainly originate further south so, at least initially, it is worth looking there to see the significance of the colour red. In the eastern Mediterranean we do find a few plants other than poppies with similar-coloured flowers, such as the crown anemone, *Anemone coronaria*, turban buttercup, *Ranunculus asiaticus*, three species of pheasant's-eye, *Adonis* spp., and some tulips, *Tulipa* spp. Red flowers are still unusual in the flora as a whole, and comprise no more than 2 per cent of species, but several of these are common.[1] Since they all have medium or large bowl-shaped red flowers, they form a very visible part of the flora. Their similarity

Utagawa Hiroshige,
*Poppy and Sparrow*, c. 1830,
woodblock print. The
inscription reads: 'Poppy
flowers are so delicate
that if a bird flies near
them their petals might
come off.'

## *Three Sisters*, an Israeli fairy tale[2]

Once upon a time, in a far country, there lived a handsome prince.

After years of dissipation and tumultuous bachelorhood the Prince decided to take a woman in his life, and announced that he would give an evening of 'speed dating', free and open to the female audience.

Hundreds of women decided to try their luck, including the Three Sisters: Anemone, Scarlet Crowfoot (Ranunculus) and Poppy.

On the appointed day the sisters (like most invited) stormed the nearby mall to get the most up-to-date garment and the most impressive accessories. The mall was full of women pushing and shopping to get an outfit. Within minutes the sisters had lost each other and only met again when they returned to their homes, each with the result of her shopping frenzy, all with the same red dress.

Trouble! How could the Prince distinguish between the three?

After the tears, the blood returned to their faces, and they found a solution: each of them would add a rather unique accessory to her red dress.

Anemone added a white scarf she brought from her travels in India.

Scarlet Crowfoot, the trendy, added a green belt, decorated her dress with glitters and put on glossy lipstick.

Poppy wore a black beaded necklace around her neck.

With the upgraded performance they entered the hall and seized the Prince's heart within minutes. He spent an entire day with every one of them, and after three days he admitted he could not reach a decision. The three sisters were also captured by the Prince's charms, and each wanted him for herself.

Wow, and another solution was found: the Prince would marry the three of them, on condition that once a year, every year, he should dedicate a period of time to each one separately.

The Prince in love quickly agreed, and only asked the sisters to continue to wear their special accessories to avoid unnecessary confusion and shame. For the same reason he also decided to open a logbook and to set dates for each sister, in alphabetical order – Anemone, Scarlet Crowfoot, Poppy. Since then, every year, Anemone is the first to bloom, with a white scarf around the stamens, Scarlet Crowfoot with the bright shiny leaves and the typically green sepals enclosing the petals in the form of a belt, is the second to appear and Poppy finishes the cycle, with dark circles on the petals.

So now you can distinguish the difference between an anemone and a poppy.

suggests that they have actually converged in colour and shape. This has given rise to a modern Israeli fairy tale distinguishing the species. It is, perhaps, somewhat contrived as a tale and written for visiting botanists, but it does neatly distinguish the three most common and similar species of red flower that grow in Israel. Here, what is normally referred to as the turban buttercup is called the scarlet crowfoot/buttercup.

❦

A flower may look strikingly beautiful to us, but this is, of course, incidental to its main function, which is to enable pollination so that it can set seed. The pollination of flowers has been the subject of a great deal of study ever since the early civilizations of the Middle East and Egypt realized that date palms needed pollinating. The idea of the cooperation between a flower and an insect, especially in a rather competitive world, has great appeal.

All these red flowers are large and showy, indicating that, at least in part, they must be reliant on pollinating animals. In Europe, that means insects. The floral display and the presentation of pollen as a reward clearly indicate that the flower is adapted for insect pollin-ation. It is possible that there could be some other way of transferring pollen such as the wind, even though wind pollination at first glance seems unlikely: wind-pollinated flowers are generally small, incon-spicuous, often green or brownish. They have plenty of dry pollen that disperses in the wind and a feathery stigma. Obvious examples are most of our trees and all our grasses, as hay fever sufferers will know well.[3] Poppies, with their showy flowers, are clearly not in this category, but they do produce a lot of pollen, and some will almost certainly disperse in the wind. This may well reach a stigma in places where a population is dense. Likewise, if a large animal, such as a cow or a deer, passes by and its fur brushes a poppy it could easily carry some pollen to another plant and pollinate it. In dense populations of poppies, large mammals and wind could even be important as pollinating agents. But insects must be much more important than either of these; the flowers are clearly pollinated mainly by insects.

In the eastern Mediterranean these red, bowl-shaped flowers all attract a range of insects but it seems that several species of specialist flower-visiting beetles in the genus *Amphicoma* in the Scarabaeidae are the most numerous and important pollinators. Some solitary bees have also been recorded as effective pollinators. We do not usually think of beetles as being important flower visitors and, indeed, some beetles can have damaging effects, feeding on flowers and even breeding in them without transferring pollen to any great extent. Although bees, butterflies, moths and flies are the most important insect pollinators in nearly all parts of the world, beetles are of significant, though minor, importance in the warmer regions, including the eastern Mediterranean.

Insects have compound eyes that are very different in form from those of humans, relying on a large number of small 'ocelli', each polarizing the light, allowing the insect to establish a picture from the combination. Only some insects can distinguish colours; among those that can, colour discrimination is different in different groups. Beetles can discriminate between colours, and are unusual among insects in being able to distinguish red colours fairly well.[4] This could well give red beetle-pollinated flowers a particular advantage, as the colour will attract beetles but not other insects that might otherwise take the plant's resources without pollinating the flowers successfully. One may argue that this is the reason for the evolution of the red colour of the petals. Whatever the reason, it seems as if these different plant species have converged in colour and in the bowl-shaped form of their flowers.

When an insect finds a productive flower it establishes a 'search-image' to find it again. This is advantageous to the insect as it can save energy in its searches. With similar-looking flowers blooming at different times of year, parcelling out the spring flowering season between them, the search image remains. A plant's pollen is transferred to other individuals of the same species, but without too

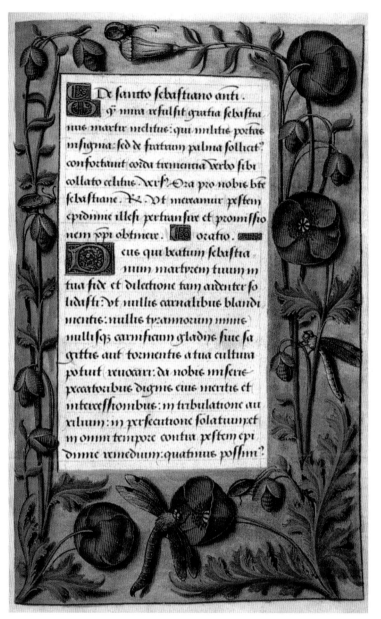

The poppy, in John Gerard's *Herball, or Generall Historie of Plantes* (1597).

much pollen going to the wrong species. As the Israeli tale relates, the poppies are the last of the group to flower, in May, before the summer drought sets in.

Flower-visiting beetles are common in the Mediterranean but they are much rarer further north. As the poppy spread north in Europe it seems to have left its beetle pollinators behind, coming to rely more on bees.

At this point we find in the corn poppy colour a fascinating detail that is not visible to the human eye. Corn poppy flowers have more than one colour pigment in their petals. There are numerous flower colour pigments known, many of which are chemically very similar in structure, even though different chemical variants reflect different colours ranging from purple or blue to reds, oranges or yellows. In northern Europe the corn poppy has a particular combination of pigments that reflects in two quite separate parts of the light spectrum. The red that we see is a reflection of the longest wavelengths of light that our eyes are sensitive to. Poppies absorb the light in the rest of the visible spectrum so we see the flowers as red. But poppies in northern Europe also reflect in the near ultraviolet – that part of the spectrum immediately next to the violet with wavelengths shorter than any we can detect. It is most unusual for plant petals to reflect in the ultraviolet and not to reflect in the violet and blue part of the visual spectrum as well, but northern poppies do.[5]

There is another twist in this tale of colour. Extraordinarily, the poppy has this extra pigment only in northern Europe, and not in its original native area of the eastern Mediterranean. If we assume that the poppy only spread through northern Europe with agriculture, it is clear that this is a development that happened, at most, about 10,000 years ago. There is a transitional area, however, with some poppy populations in Greece and other parts of southeastern Europe having a mixture of plants with ultraviolet reflectance, plants without it and some intermediates in the same populations.[6]

As far as we know, none of the corn poppy's closest relatives in the eastern Mediterranean reflect in the ultraviolet, and none of the three other British red poppies do either. It appears to be something unique to the corn poppy, although it is the best studied of all the poppies and further study may turn up another.

Pollination has been extremely well studied in northern Europe. There was a surge of interest during the nineteenth century, including many contributions by Charles Darwin and Sir John Lubbock (Lord Avebury) in Britain. The greatest compilation of this work was done in Germany by Paul Knuth in his huge *Handbook of Flower Pollination* of 1906–9, based especially on work by a fellow German, Hermann Müller, but including Lubbock's observations too.[7] Knuth detailed the flower visitors to many of the plants of Germany, most of which occur also in Britain. Knuth's compendium recorded at least twelve species of bee visiting poppies in northern Europe: the honeybee, two species of bumblebee and some solitary bees, plus several flies including three species of hoverfly, and three species of beetle, all collecting pollen. In addition, the occasional grasshopper and earwig were recorded resting on the flowers. The bees were the most numerous and important pollinators. McNaughton and Harper added to the list but showed that the solitary bees were the most important visitors.[8]

The extra pigment reflecting ultraviolet light, in poppies from northern Europe, starts to make sense in the light of which insects are the most important pollinators. Bees are sensitive to the near ultraviolet that we cannot see but, unlike beetles, cannot discriminate red colours clearly. The result is that we see poppies as bright scarlet, as we cannot see any of the ultraviolet reflectance; bees see them as ultraviolet with perhaps a tinge from the red. Detailed experimental study on colour preference by bees generally, using coloured paper and not flowers, is reported by Knuth. The fact that many flowers reflect or absorb in the ultraviolet was not known in his time, so the experiments only cover that part of the spectrum visible to humans: 'The following series, therefore, gives the colours that are appreciated by the honey-bee in the order of preference    saturated blue, violet, blue, red, white and pale yellow, pure green, glaring red and glaring yellow.' The poppy comes in the 'glaring red' category as a colour of lowest preference. Knuth had not realized that poppies reflected ultraviolet as well as red, so must have seen the poppy as having a very surprising colour for a plant dependent on bees for pollination. We now know that we can add near ultraviolet to the list, as one of the most attractive colours for bees to visit, and the reflectance pattern of the poppy makes sense.

Frequently, though far from always, the corn poppy and other poppies have a black centre to the flower. This is a region at the base of the petals that absorbs the light, including the ultraviolet light. Such a dark centre is a common marker for visiting insects, indicating where the reward is. It occurs in many plant species but when they only absorb in the ultraviolet we cannot detect the difference. More flowers have dark centres to visiting bees than the ones that we can see.

It is worth noting that white flowers, of which there are a particularly large number in the British flora, reflect all the wavelengths of light that are visible to us, but this is not including their colour patterns in the near ultraviolet. If we look at the plants with white flowers in our flora from a bee's-eye view, we find there are differences in colour between different species. Some absorb in the near ultraviolet or part of it, meaning that bees would see a coloured flower. Others reflect the ultraviolet as well as the other wavelengths, rendering them 'white' to bees as well as to us.

The corn poppy is unusual among agricultural weeds in that it cannot fertilize itself so must have an external agent to transfer pollen. It is highly likely that the appearance of the new pigment being attractive to bees seriously facilitated the spread of the corn poppy outside the range of its beetle pollinators, and contributed to its position as the most commonly found poppy in Europe.

The other red poppy species of northern Europe can all fertilize themselves, though they do attract insect visitors at times. The corn poppy has been known, rarely, to cross with the long-headed poppy to produce a sterile hybrid.

## Some Other Red Flowers

The red colour of poppy flowers is unusual in northern Europe but not quite unique. There are two other plants in the British flora with genuinely bright red flowers. Like the poppy, both are short-lived annuals of disturbed ground, though both are smaller than the poppy and neither is related to it.

The first is the scarlet pimpernel, *Anagallis arvensis*, in the primrose family (Primulaceae), sometimes known as the 'poor-man's weather-glass' after its habit of closing up in cool or shady weather. It can be common, especially on chalky soil, and grows in agricultural fields and sometimes in gardens. It now has an almost worldwide distribution on disturbed land, but originated in Europe. In Britain it is probably an archaeophyte, like the poppy.[9] Its flowers are usually a pale scarlet, with a purple centre, though variants with blue

Scarlet pimpernel, *Anagallis arvensis*, in Normandy.

or pink flowers occur in places. It is fairly small and inconspicuous, despite its striking colour (*The Scarlet Pimpernel* became well known as the title of a play of 1903, and subsequent novel by Baroness Orczy, about the French Revolution, the name being the nickname of her subversive aristocrat Sir Percy Blakeney, whose calling card depicted the flower.)

The other red plant is the pheasant's-eye, *Adonis annua*, a member of the buttercup family, a cornfield weed but a very rare one and, again, an archaeophyte brought in with cultivation.[10] It derives its English name from the striking resemblance of its flower to the eye of a pheasant, surrounded as it is by naked red skin. In fact this plant may have gone completely extinct in Britain with the decline of so many cornfield weeds during the twentieth century, but has now been reintroduced and is maintained in a few places.

Pheasant's-eye, *Adonis annua*, Buckinghamshire.

Red helleborine,
*Cephalanthera rubra*,
Cévennes, France.

The other flowers in our flora that are named, or sometimes described, as red are all of a very different hue, usually a purplish pink, such as the red campion, red clover, red bartsia, red dead-nettle and the rare red helleborine. Sorrels and docks may have dull red parts on their otherwise greenish, fairly inconspicuous flowers that are largely wind-pollinated. There are a few plants with red flowers that have naturalized in Britain. Fuchsia, first introduced from South America in 1788, is now widespread near western coasts. Two species of peony with deep-red flowers come from the central and western Mediterranean. Both are rarely naturalized, one long-established on Steep Holm in the Bristol Channel, the other appearing casually when thrown out of gardens. The Maltese cross, a red-flowered campion native to Russia, is long established in Bristol.

## The Advantages of Being Red

The poppy, the pheasant's-eye and the scarlet pimpernel are all common in the Mediterranean and probably developed their red colour in this region and colonized northwards. If so, all are likely to be mainly pollinated by beetles in their original range. Insect visitors to the pheasant's-eye or scarlet pimpernel in northern Europe are rare, with only the occasional honeybee and a few flies recorded collecting pollen.[11] Both plants are largely self-pollinated in northern Europe. Neither has any ultraviolet-reflecting pigment. As for the extra ultraviolet pigment in northern European corn poppies, we must suppose that this developed after it spread northwards with agriculture from its native eastern Mediterranean.

There is one other reference to the importance of the poppy's colour. This has never been followed up and is unlikely to be of great importance, but the idea dates back to the nineteenth century and is reported by Knuth in his *Handbook* from 1906:

> Hermann Müller regards the glowing red hue of the
> Papaver Rhoeas not only as serving to allure insects,
> but also as a terrifying or defensive colour, by which
> grazing animals are made aware of the poisonous
> juices of the flower, so that they avoid it. As evidence
> of this assumption, Müller notes that on the 'Kampen'
> (i.e. the enclosed meadows near Lippstadt, on which
> the cows pass the whole summer) the flowers of the
> corn-poppy remain untouched, while almost all others
> are grazed down.

Many grazing animals are adept at recognizing poisonous plants anyway – for example, avoiding the highly poisonous ragwort – and the animals will need to avoid the poppy before the flowers appear. So Müller's idea seems unlikely, despite the fact that we see red as the colour of danger, and mammals are particularly sensitive to red.

Some other parts of the world have many red-flowered plants, especially the tropics and the temperate regions of the southern hemisphere and, to an extent, North America too. Some of these will grow in our gardens and a few, like the fuchsia, can spread. The reason seems clear: red flowers are attractive to bird pollinators and not to the main pollinators of northern Europe and Asia – the bees, butterflies, moths and flies. In Europe and northern Asia no birds are specialist pollinators, although some birds do visit flowers regularly and may transfer pollen – a good example being the blue tit systematically visiting willow catkins and collecting and transferring willow pollen on the head feathers.[12]

In those parts of the world with numerous red flowers there are specialist bird pollinators, including the large families of hummingbirds in the Americas, sunbirds in Africa and southern Asia, honeyeaters in Australasia and other smaller families in various parts of the world. Birds' eyes are sensitive to red, like human eyes, though they have some sensitivity to the near ultraviolet too. Red flowers may have appeared where birds are specialist pollinators, at least in part because many insects cannot distinguish red clearly and, as we have seen, it is a colour of low preference for honeybees. Birds are the most effective pollinators of many red-flowered plants, and if insects remove the pollen or nectar the flowers may become less attractive to the birds. Red becomes a good colour for these plants because it is less attractive to the insects.[13] Having said all that, in my own garden I have noticed many bees visiting the red flowers of both fuchsia, originally from South America, and *Grevillea rosmarinifolia*, originally from Australia, even though both are pollinated mainly by birds in their native lands. Both produce abundant nectar, and clearly bees can find them despite their colour.

Corn poppy flowers opening: sepals splitting at tip (top)
and sepals breaking off at base.

*four*
# The Life Cycle of the Poppy

T he poppy produces hermaphrodite flowers, with functional male and female parts in each flower. Around 80 per cent of all flowering plants are hermaphrodite; the others have unisexual flowers either on the same plant, like many trees, or on different plants, like holly and stinging nettles, or some combination of male, female and hermaphrodite flowers. These fertile parts are surrounded by four petals, though the occasional flower may have more, in two whorls of two and two sepals surrounding these when in bud. These two green sepals protect the flower in bud. As the flower stem grows, the buds of most poppies are on nodding stems. The stem straightens as the flower opens. At this stage the sepals may open up as the petals expand, as with most flowers, but frequently they break off at the base and then can often remain perched on the top of the expanding petals for a short time. From either position they drop off as the flower opens fully.

The petals of poppies are mostly thin and rather silky in texture and many, including those of the corn poppy, are somewhat translucent. One of their features, and one that is often mentioned in the literature, is their crumpled appearance as they expand. This is more obvious in poppies than in most plants because of the size of the flower compared with the bud, and the texture of the petals themselves. If the sepals remain on top of the expanding petals this serves to keep the crushed appearance as they expand. John Ruskin's description of the poppy flower in his extraordinary book *Proserpina*, of 1888 (discussed in more depth in Chapter Five), is particularly evocative: 'The two imprisoning green leaves [sepals] are shaken to the ground; the aggrieved corolla [petals] smooths itself in the sun and comforts itself as it can; but remains visibly crushed and hurt to the end of its days.'

There are numerous stamens in each flower, producing large quantities of pollen which, in corn poppies and other red poppies, varies from dark brown to a dark blue-purple that looks almost black. There are usually about ten carpels, the female parts of the flower, in corn poppies, each with a stigma, but this can vary from five to sixteen. The long-headed usually has seven or eight. Other poppies, such as the oriental poppy, have more. The ovaries below are fused and these will eventually form the dry capsule that is the poppy fruit. Inside each carpel is a large number of ovules. In poppies

Open flower showing dark stamens.

there is no nectar; the reward for the insects is pollen. Pollen can be a vital protein source for visiting insects, and they will visit poppy flowers to collect the copious pollen.[1]

There is some disagreement about the scent of a poppy. Most agree that there is, in fact, no scent at all, but John Clare wrote, in 'May' of his *Shepherd's Calendar* of 1827: 'Corn-poppies, that in crimson dwell, / Call'd "Headach's" for their sickly smell . . .'. Knuth tells us in one place that there is no odour but, later, that it has an 'unpleasant poppy-odour'. The slightest trace of a bitter odour is perhaps occasionally present, most likely in warm weather, bringing off traces of the drugs that are present in the plant as a whole. 'Headache', or sometimes 'Headwark', and 'Earache' are old country names, stemming from an early belief that smelling the poppies causes such aches, and perhaps Clare is simply recording this. It is a persistent belief, with perhaps its best-known cultural reference in *The Wizard of Oz* where Dorothy and her dog Toto fall asleep in a field of poppies.

Corn poppies cannot normally fertilize themselves. When the flowers first open, the pollen has often already been shed and may be seen on the petals and stigmas. It was supposed by earlier authors that they could and would fertilize themselves. Poppies have a mechanism known as self-incompatibility in which a plant's own pollen is recognized in the stigma or style and stopped from growing down to fertilize the seeds. It means that any one plant can fertilize or be fertilized by most other plants in the population, but not itself. Most cornfield weeds are capable of self-fertilization. This can have great advantages in such situations where speed of the life cycle is most important – they must complete their life cycle before the plough comes back. This means that it will be advantageous for the flowers to open at a young age, often at an early developmental stage when still quite small. Nearly all of these self-fertilizing weeds have small flowers. Only small amounts of pollen will be needed and all aspects of flowering and fruit set can happen quickly as no external agent is needed for seed set. Opening at this early stage also subverts any system of self-incompatibility such as that found in the poppy.

There are two main advantages of cross-fertilization. Firstly, it throws up a greater variety of offspring and this may allow the plants to adapt better to changing conditions or evolve resistance to disease. Secondly, it avoids 'inbreeding depression', the weakness that may come from both parents having the same genetic form for each trait. Cross-fertilized plants are likely to outcompete self-fertilized ones, but in agricultural fields competition between plants may well be of lesser importance than in most other habitats. There will be plenty of nutrients available and much bare ground. In these circumstances, speed of growth and reproduction is likely to be the most important advantage for a plant.

It is interesting in this situation that the poppy is self-incompatible, produces a large showy flower and needs to spread its pollen to other plants to set seeds. It appears to combine speed of growth and successful pollination with cross-fertilization. The only other common cornfield weed that is self-incompatible is the charlock, *Sinapis arvensis*. It may not be coincidental that, of all the short-lived annual weeds of cornfields, these two weeds are now two of the commonest and largest. The variation thrown up with the constant cross-fertilization may allow them to adapt better than those that are predominantly self-fertilizing.

Self-incompatibility has been studied in a range of plants, and in the great majority, including the corn poppy, it seems that one highly variable gene is responsible for this recognition. Successful pollen needs to come from another plant that does not share the same form of this gene.[2] This means that there is usually incompatibility with the plant's own close relatives too. The number of forms (alleles) of this gene in corn poppies varies, but in a study on three different populations, there turned out to be a total of 45 different alleles, fifteen of them in common between all three populations. Many of these alleles are widely distributed right across the whole range of the species, so that there may be fewer than seventy in the species as a whole.[3]

Poppies have what appears to be an unusual system of self-incompatibility. When its own pollen germinates on a stigma, a

Ripe capsule of long-headed poppy showing holes at the top of each ovary from which the seeds are shed.

chemical process is triggered, usually within five minutes, that leads to 'programmed cell death', stopping the growth of the pollen tube and then killing the pollen.[4] In most other self-incompatible plants the tube is simply blocked or slowed down and there is no programmed cell death. The poppy's self-incompatibility system is undoubtedly 'leaky' and a few individuals will be capable of self-fertilization, but cross-fertilization is the norm. The long-headed and the other British poppies can fertilize themselves.[5]

The fruit of all members of the poppy family is a dry capsule, usually containing numerous seeds. When ripe a small hole opens up at the top of each ovary. Each hole has a band on top of it, the bands deriving from the stigmas so the number of bands is the same as the number of ovaries. In the corn poppy, once the flower is fertilized, seeds are produced in great quantity and shed from the capsules through the holes. The seeds are tiny, each weighing about 0.1 milligram, and a capsule produces, on average, more than 1,300 seeds. Overall a really large plant could produce up to 300,000 seeds in its one growing season; 30,000–50,000 is normal for any well-grown plant.[6] The stem of the plant is thin and wiry and is constantly bowing and flexing in the wind, so the seeds can be shed effectively, often likened to spreading pepper from a pepper pot. The seeds of the opium poppy are slightly larger than those of the corn poppy and rich in oil. They can be produced in large quantity too and are familiar as the bluish condiment added to breads and other foods. They do not contain any appreciable quantity of the narcotics for which the plant is famous.

The other species of poppy in the genera *Papaver* and *Meconopsis* have similar dry capsules with holes or slits near the top, but within the rest of the family the fruit is quite variable and one of the main diagnostic features of the different genera. The yellow horned poppy has long thin capsules that split from the tip; the California poppy splits from the base; and some other poppies split explosively, flinging their seeds out in a similar way to the gorse.[7]

The lightness of the seeds means they can be carried by the wind to an extent, but most will fall quickly and, in the corn poppy and others with no explosive dispersal, probably all land initially within 2 m (6.5 ft) of the parent plant. They have no other means of immediate dispersal, but they do have one feature that can lead to chance dispersal over a much greater distance: the seeds are potentially long-lived. When first shed they are not fully mature and they require burial in the soil before they can germinate. Once fully mature they can live for decades. Various records have been kept on the longevity of the seeds and the results have shown some variation, with an annual death rate of 9 to 40 per cent. A 'half-life' – the length of time until half have died – has been recorded as around ten years but some can live for fifty years, or possibly eighty.[8] The numbers of seeds in the soil seed bank can be enormous, with estimates of up to twenty million poppy seeds per hectare in suitable fields. This means that, even after many years and with a very small percentage of viable seeds, a field can still be covered with poppies if conditions are favourable. It also means that chance movement, on the feet of

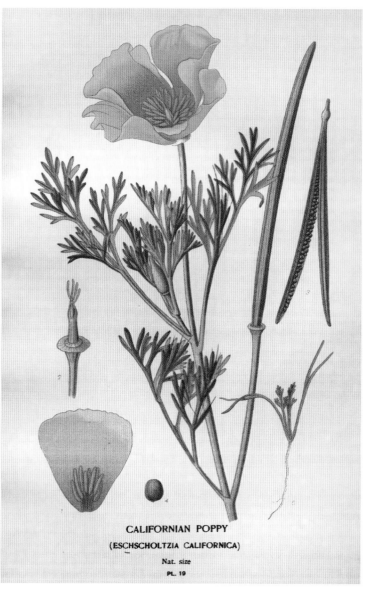

**CALIFORNIAN POPPY**

(ESCHSCHOLTZIA CALIFORNICA)

Nat. size

PL. 19

'Californian poppy' with pod shown splitting from base.

animals, by strong winds or floods long after the seeds are first shed, can lead to effective long-distance dispersal.

The seedlings, like other agricultural weeds, have a requirement for light before they will germinate.[9] In addition, once mature, they need temperatures above about 15°C (59°F) during the day and 4°C (39°F) at night. A plough will frequently bring buried seed of many agricultural weeds into the light, and germination can come after a fairly brief exposure. Some farmers plough mainly in the dark to avoid the germination of unwanted weeds.

In Britain and northern Europe, seedling poppies emerge usually between February and April and start to flower around the middle of June with a peak of flowering towards the end of June into early July. Flowering gradually tails off after that but can continue sporadically until October. In some years there is a second, smaller, flush of seedling germination in late summer and these seedlings can overwinter to flower the following summer. Seeds are normally set within four weeks of the flower opening. In the southern part of its range growth is earlier and it flowers in May before the summer drought sets in.

The time of germination can make a considerable difference to the success of the plant. In the long-headed poppy, *Papaver dubium*, autumn seedlings emerging from non-dormant seeds have high winter mortality in some years, but if they survive, they produce up to ten times as many seeds as those that germinate in spring. Other poppies are likely to be similar.

## five

# The Poppy as a Symbol of Agriculture

༄

There is no other plant that so completely reminds us of our farmland. But it is really the farmland of our parents or grandparents, the generations before about 1960, when poppies still frequently coloured the landscape. This makes us realize what has happened to our rural environment in the last fifty years or so. The poppy is still common in places, but today it has become a plant of the edges of fields, or of field headlands deliberately left as a conservation measure, or roadsides, building sites and other patches of disturbed soil. Only rarely do we see it covering a field, and then usually it is a field that has been abandoned by agriculture, at least temporarily.

We have constantly been trying to find ways to increase crop yields and reduce competition from weeds and insect pests. Intensification of agriculture is not a new development. In Britain the Enclosure Acts that ran through Parliament, mainly between 1760 and 1820, were one major change. Some of our cornfield weeds must have had a steep decline at that time, though many had been declining slowly before that as agricultural methods slowly improved. Despite this, many weeds, the poppy pre-eminent among them, remained common.

Another major change came after the Second World War, with the advent of mass mechanized and chemical agriculture that spread across much of Europe, mainly in the 1960s. Hedges were destroyed, fields became bigger – often much bigger – and insecticides and herbicides were spread on the fields like never before. Some of these pesticides have since been banned because of the damage done to the wildlife, most famously by the organochlorines like DDT. In recent years the allocation of most pesticides has become more focused, primarily with cost in mind. Against the wildlife, pesticides have been all too successful. Most of our fields have become true mono-cultures, with only the crop present and no weeds at all.

All our cornfield weeds have become much rarer. Some have been completely extinguished from Britain, such as swine's succory, thorow-wax and probably corn cockle and pheasant's-eye, though

Swine's succory,
a cornfield weed
extinct in Britain,
found in Cévennes,
France.

Corn cockle in Cambridgeshire, a classic cornfield weed now confined
to conservation areas where it has been reintroduced and maintained.

these have been reintroduced.[1] We have also lost many insects,
including most of the butterflies from huge areas of agricultural
land, and numerous birds, such as corn buntings and turtle doves.[2]
It has become an event to see many of these species. They hang
on around edges and margins, but mainly those deliberately left for
wildlife. Agricultural land has become a desert for wildlife across
large swathes of the country, with benefits for crop yield, and a huge
loss in biodiversity. The heart of the countryside has gone. It has
truly been stolen from us and what was, for centuries, the 'common
ground' for us all has ceased to be so.[3] With that loss has come the
loss of interest in and knowledge of the natural world. Nobody
walks for pleasure in the sterile environment of agricultural fields
any more. Even the soil has gone, its nutrients that had been laid
down for centuries and added to with organic manure, replaced by
chemical fertilizers.

A look at the *Farmers Weekly* of 5 September 2014 shows that,
despite the immense success of intensive agriculture, farmers are still
worried about poppies. One headline stated 'Herbicide Resistant
Poppies Mean Trouble for Growers', with warnings of another

Corn buttercup or 'devil's claw', now rare as a cornfield weed, Cévennes, France.

'black-grass disaster'. They are concerned about poppies becoming increasingly resistant to one of the most widely used types of herbicide based on sulfonylurea.[4]

A few of our cornfield weeds are thought to be native in disturbed places such as sand dunes, but many will have spread into Britain and northern Europe with agriculture a few thousand years ago. All of them must have increased enormously with agriculture. Whatever their origin, we have lived with them for thousands of years and they are part of our heritage. As the plants with which we were most familiar, they have become part of the fabric of the country and were once a feature of many people's daily lives. This is reflected in the evocative names we have for many, such as corn marigold, Venus' looking-glass, shepherd's needle and devil's claw (or corn butter-cup), as well as those already mentioned. Their beauty did not escape farmers even if they did spend time and effort eradicating them from their fields. Their loss is a warning to us of our potentially too great power to manipulate our environment for our own use. As so often, we discover our affections for things only when we are losing them. The conservation of cornfield weeds is a particularly intractable problem because of where they grow, but conserve them we must even if it is only in designated places. Nature reserves or conservation field boundaries may not be entirely 'authentic' environments, but they have to be better than losing these weeds altogether.[5]

There are changes afoot, and there has been something of a national reaction against some of the chemical onslaught. This came initially from those concerned for the beauty of the countryside and about the loss of diversity. Rachel Carson alerted the world to the dangers of pesticides with her 1962 book, evocatively entitled *Silent Spring*, leading to bans on DDT and other pesticides in many countries.[6] More problems with pesticides are gradually coming to light, such as the systemic insecticides collectively known as neonicotinoids, which have been blamed in the last couple of years for the huge decline in bee populations and those of other insects.

As well as threatening the insects or other pests they are designed to kill, many pesticides are now seen as potentially dangerous for humans. Most recently the widely used glyphosate weed-killer, marketed as 'Roundup' by the giant pharmaceutical company Monsanto, has come in for serious criticism. It is strongly associated with genetic modification, as 'Roundup-ready' varieties of maize, rape and other crops have been genetically modified to be resistant to this herbicide. There has been research and testing on 'Roundup-ready' wheat, although as of 2015 it is not commercially available. It all becomes a little sinister when you learn that the GM seeds are also sold by Monsanto and the plants are sterile so farmers need to buy new seeds each year rather than save any. Monsanto get a double profit, selling the GM crops and the herbicide together. There is mounting evidence that glyphosate is carcinogenic or tumour-causing and, although it can be inactive in the soil as it becomes bound to the soil particles, it can persist in the environment for a year or more.[7]

There have long been schemes promoting wildlife on farms. The Farming and Wildlife Advisory Group was set up in the 1960s and still provides advice on environmentally friendly measures. Now there are several governmental schemes such as the Environmentally

Sensitive Area Scheme that started in 1987 and its successor, the Environmental Stewardship Scheme, now administered by Natural England. The Soil Association has effectively promoted 'organic' agriculture to the point where there is organic food in all the main supermarkets across much of Europe. This emphasis in recent years has led to some limited changes in agricultural land, and some local reversal of the trends towards rarity of our cornfield weeds and animals, but it remains very local and patchy.

The poppy has become much rarer during the agrochemical onslaught of the last sixty years or so, but its combination of seed longevity, late germination in the spring and fast growth and seed setting has meant that it has proved itself one of the more resilient of weeds. Our very gradual and local change in attitudes towards the environment has led to a minor turnaround in the fortunes of agricultural weeds in places, and the poppy has benefited from this. But it is unlikely that the poppy will ever return to anything close to its abundance of earlier times. Fields covered with poppies are likely to remain a rare sight. Many people born after about 1970 may never have seen such a field. The poppy has survived, even though it is mostly survival on the edges, as a marginal plant. If this had always been the case, I doubt it would ever have caught the public imagination in the way it has. We would not be likely to have it as the signature colour of cornfields, nor as the potent symbol that it has become, especially of war and remembrance.

## Early References to Poppies

Ancient civilizations cultivated the ground, and the corn poppy became a cornfield weed early on, but it seems that, right from the start, the corn poppy and the opium poppy became mixed up in people's imaginations. The corn poppy rapidly became a symbol of agriculture and fertility, the opium poppy of sleep, hallucination and, perhaps, death, but it is not always clear which one is being referred to. Normally the likelihood is that if the flowers are depicted it will be the corn poppy, and if the seed-pods are depicted the reference will be to opium. But they have been confused and considered together so often, and in so many contexts, that it is frequently impossible to tell which is being discussed.

Both poppy species probably have their origin in the eastern Mediterranean and southwestern Asia and, with Mesopotamia the site of the earliest agriculture, under the Sumerians, the people will have been familiar with both corn and opium poppies, and several others besides. Written records of the Sumerians are rather fragmentary but their goddess of harvest, Nimasa (or Nimada), appears in sketches holding what appear to be poppy capsules, perhaps the corn poppy, as it is a symbol of the harvest. By the time the Assyrians were in the ascendant in the same region between about 2000 BC and 600 BC we have more written records. There have also been some Assyrian bas-reliefs found dating from around 700 BC, one of which appears to show a religious leader holding poppy seed-heads – this time it is surely opium.[8]

The ancient Greeks and Romans knew much about the properties of both corn poppies and opium poppies and incorporated them into their myths. In his *Greek Myths*, Robert Graves thought that the poppy with its scarlet colour might be a symbol of resurrection, similar to what it became in association with the First World War, but the evidence here is fairly scant.[9]

The strongest association in ancient Greece, and subsequently Rome, is with the goddess of fertility, known as Demeter in Greek, Ceres in Latin, from which we get our word cereal. She teaches mankind the art of cultivating cereals, mainly wheat and barley, harvesting them, threshing out the grain and making flour and bread. She also shows them how to draw boundaries and take possession of an area. She weeps for the loss of her beloved daughter Persephone/Proserpine who has been taken into the underworld by Hades/Pluto. While Persephone is imprisoned in the underworld, the seasons stop and it takes the intervention of Zeus' messenger, Hermes, to get Hades to agree to release her back to her mother for two-thirds of

'Genie' holding poppy capsules, from a relief of the palace
of King Sargon II, Assyria (present-day Iraq), c. 700 BC.

Roman statue of Ceres holding a poppy capsule in her right hand.

Poppies in Demeter's lap, on the Ara Pacis in Rome.

the year. For the other months, while she is in the underworld, the ground remains infertile. This barren period is the Mediterranean summer drought. When Persephone returns to the world in the autumn it is time to sow crops. The Romans probably changed Persephone's name to the similar Proserpine or Proserpina because the Latin *proserpere* means to emerge. In the nineteenth century John Ruskin used the name *Proserpina* for his plant book that featured the poppy with particular prominence.

The main emblem associated with Demeter/Ceres appears to be wheat but the poppy is frequently associated with the goddess too, and she can be depicted with bunches of wheat and poppies in her hands.[10] In Roman times Ceres was depicted with a garland of poppies around her head and such garlands were placed on statues of her. There are coins with poppies depicted on them from various parts of the Roman Empire, usually in association with wheatsheafs as symbols of fertility and agriculture. One Roman myth suggests that flowers were never used by the people in their sacrifices to Ceres, as Proserpine was taken from her while picking flowers, but Jupiter allowed Ceres her poppies. Poppies appear to have a dual function, as they so often do. They can be depicted with Ceres as capsules, the opium providing comfort to Ceres' grief at the loss of

Proserpine, but also as the flower of cornfields and as symbols of the fertility of the soil.

Another Greek myth surrounding poppies is that they first appeared from the tears of Aphrodite as she wept for the loss of her beloved Adonis. As is common in the history of the poppy in culture, it is not entirely clear whether these were opium poppies or corn poppies.

## The Poppy Symbol in Folklore

There is much folklore associated with the poppy, nearly all of it to do with the harvest.[11] Fields full of poppies were seen as the lifeblood of the field, a confirmation of its fertility, reflecting the classical myths about the plants. In many parts of Britain it was considered unlucky to pick a poppy, and children were warned never to do so, especially when the crop was growing, since it would cause a thunderstorm, hence the various 'thunder' names. Anything that might promote thunderstorms was clearly to be avoided as, though a common feature of the summer months, a vigorous storm can flatten a crop. The connection with thunderstorms could be reversed, as so often in folklore; poppies and other weeds placed under the eaves of a house were said to be protection from lightning, though woe betide anyone if the petals fell off during the picking – this would imply that lightning was going to strike that household. In traditions and customs, midsummer's day has always been special. This turning point of the year has given rise to numerous rituals, a few of which continue to this day, mainly with latter-day druids. Any agricultural weeds, and especially poppies, that had been weeded out before then were burned on a ritual pyre. This symbolized resurrection and ensured a good harvest.

Poppies are said to cause headaches if you smell them, but this too has its reverse – the poppy also used to be seen as a cure for headaches (maybe it is this kind of folklore that led to our modern homoeopathic remedies). There is some truth in the ancient story:

the corn poppy does have a mild sedative and analgesic property, although nowhere near as strong as that of the opium poppy.

A few other associations have been made, at times. Staring too long at a poppy was meant to make you blind, hence the 'blind' names. Poppy petals were among those that could be plucked by young maidens to be placed in the hollow of her hand. If there was a loud report when it was struck by the other hand, her lover would be true to her. The connection with blood is obvious and the old 'soldier' folk names show that the connection dates back much further than the First World War. The old Cornish name of wartflower suggests that the latex of poppies was used to treat warts, as that of its relative, the greater celandine, has been.

Weeds generally were seen until recently as an inevitable and natural feature of agricultural land. In medieval times, all the living world had lessons for us from God. The poppy and other weeds were a curse on the land and could reduce harvests considerably, but they were there as a result of our sins to remind us of our fallen state.

Over the centuries, poets, other writers and painters have celebrated poppies for the spectacle of a poppy-covered field while also lamenting the effect of the poppies on crops. Prior to about 1850, most were negative about it. George Crabbe (1754–1832) is best known today as the writer of *The Borough*, a collection of poems that provided Benjamin Britten with the story for his opera *Peter Grimes*.

Elihu Vedder, *Cypresses and Poppies*, c. 1880–90, oil on canvas.

He was much admired in his day for his descriptions of rural life and, in particular, the hardships endured by the farm labourer. In his long poem *The Village* he lamented the effect of weeds on the harvest:

> Rank weeds, that every art and care defy,
> Reign o'er the land, and rob the blighted rye:
> There thistles stretch their prickly arms afar,
> And to the ragged infant threaten war;
> There poppies nodding, mock the hope of toil;

He continues in similar vein, mentioning bugloss, mallow, charlock and tare. Again, in 'The Lover's Journey' he refers to the 'dark poppy'. Crabbe clearly sees the poppy as a pest, but it is equally clear that these plants matter to him and he would expect any reader to know them. You will notice the possible association with war that he is making a century before it became a war symbol. Crabbe was a regular opium taker too.

John Clare, the great Romantic naturalist poet, constantly celebrates the beauty of the natural world and was perhaps the first to put into poetic form the fact that agricultural weeds are not mere pests. He records in *The Shepherd's Calendar* of 1827, just before the quotation about the poppy's scent (Chapter Three), that the 'weeders' meet in May and 'Ruin in the sunny hours / Full many a wild weed with its flowers.' By the second half of the nineteenth century, Romanticism had taken a serious hold on people's imaginations, largely because the ugliness of so much industry had spread rapidly, with Blake's famous 'dark Satanic mills' springing up in many places. One of Romanticism's chief protagonists was John Ruskin (1819–1900) and he has given us one of the strangest descriptions of the poppy. He was a serious naturalist as well as art critic and aesthete and some of his paintings of plants are both beautiful and botanically accurate. In 1888 he wrote what was intended as a kind of textbook of botany, *Proserpina: Studies of Wayside Flowers*, though it was not what we would consider today to be a textbook.[12] His title is taken from the Roman

John Ruskin, 'Study of Wild Rose', 1871, drawing.

myth of Proserpine. He saw plants as mainly for our edification, scientifically interesting of course but, more importantly, as things of beauty, to delight the senses and to demonstrate the presence of God. No plant was more important for this than the poppy.

In his discussion of the poppy, Ruskin laments the loss of the slow country life, especially with the coming of the railway, as the steadily increasing pace of life no longer allowed people to appreciate the beauties of nature. That is something that any naturalist today would relate to fully, as life gets ever faster, and we separate ourselves more and more completely from nature in all its beauty as well as all its difficulties. Indeed, 'biophilia', an innate love of nature, championed especially by the American zoologist Edward Wilson, is the modern term used to describe Ruskin's idea.[13] Biophilia is seen as an essential part of human nature, and without access to the natural world we run into psychological difficulties, often serious, leading to violence, crime and too much work for psychiatrists and therapists.

We have already seen Ruskin's vivid description of the unfurling of a poppy flower. He continues in a similar vein: 'It is the most transparent and delicate of all the blossoms of the field . . . always it is a flame, and warms the wind like a blown ruby.' Ruskin considered the poppy the most perfect of flowers.

D. H. Lawrence (1885–1930) was in many ways Ruskin's natural successor. He regarded the relationship between people and plants as of the highest order. In his *A Study of Thomas Hardy* of 1915, written just before the poppy became the familiar symbol of war, he saw the flower as the 'culmination and climax, the degree to be striven for' for the achievement of 'the real Me'.[14] Like Ruskin, he championed the poppy in particular:

> And I know that the common wild poppy has achieved
> so far its complete poppy-self, unquestionable. It has
> uncovered its red. Its light, its self, has risen and shone
> out, has run on the winds for a moment. It is splendid.
> The world is a world because of the poppy's red.
> Otherwise it would be a lump of clay.

In the final essay of the sequence he called *The Crown*, written just after the *Study of Thomas Hardy*, he even saw the poppy as representing God.[15]

Many poets have championed the poppy, and one of the best summaries of our ambivalent feelings towards it as an agricultural weed comes from James Stephens (1882–1950) in his poem 'In the Poppy Field' (1912):

> Mad Patsy said, he said to me,
> That every morning he could see
> An angel walking on the sky;
> Across the sunny skies of morn
> He threw great handfuls far and nigh
> Of poppy seed among the corn;
> And then, he said, the angels run
> To see the poppies in the sun.

A poppy is a devil weed,
I said to him – he disagreed;
He said the devil had no hand
In spreading flowers tall and fair
Through corn and rye and
    meadow land,
by garth and barrow everywhere:
The devil has not any flower,
But only money in his power.


And then he stretched out in the sun
And rolled upon his back for fun:
He kicked his legs and roared for joy
Because the sun was shining down:
He said he was a little boy
And would not work for any clown:
He ran and laughed behind a bee,
And danced for very ecstasy.

I suspect that nearly all of us these days, perhaps even farmers, would identify clearly with 'Mad Patsy' rather than the narrator.

Some of the best-known paintings of poppy fields are surely those of Claude Monet. The founder of Impressionism, Monet loved painting garden and agricultural landscapes. He could see the beauty in poppy fields rather than the agricultural disaster seen by Crabbe and others, perhaps seeing the natural world as the supreme gardener. His best-known painting of a poppy field, at Argenteuil, is *Les Coquelicots* of 1873. Later, at his house at Giverny, he began painting several series of the same subject, most famously those of water lilies and haystacks. One of the shortest series is three pictures of a poppy field at Giverny, painted in 1890. In all, twelve of his paintings had 'poppy' in the title and several more were agricultural landscapes with red patches indicating poppies. He clearly delighted in the play of light on the poppies within the landscape and, though they never

Claude Monet, *Coquelicots at Giverny*, 1891.

Claude Monet, *Coquelicots at Argenteuil* (Poppy Field), 1873, oil on canvas.

overwhelm any scene, they bring a brightness to it, and seem almost to shimmer in some of his paintings, especially the famous *Coquelicots at Argenteuil*.

Countryside artists, and many others, have assumed that we all have contact with fields and with poppies, but perhaps they could see

Vincent van Gogh, *Poppy Field*, 1890, oil on canvas.

that this was getting rarer in their day. So often we only appreciate particular aspects of our natural world when they are under threat or disappearing. Romantic artists of all kinds have especially depicted or written about such threatened beauty. They clearly saw the beauties of agricultural fields declining and pointed this out so clearly to the rest of us. They were sadly understating the scale of the loss; contact with such natural splendour as a poppy field is getting seriously rare and we are all diminished as a result.

# six

# The Poppy as a Symbol of War and Remembrance

If there is only one thing that a person knows about the poppy as a symbol it is its association with war and commemoration. In Britain it is impossible not to notice the poppy sellers in October and early November; or in other countries whenever remembrance is celebrated. The connection with war is clear, although exactly what that is may not be clear to some. It must be the best-known, most distinctive and probably the most successful of all street charity collections. The origins of the symbolism and the poppy selling that takes place in Britain, the USA and many Commonwealth countries, as well as, to a lesser extent, some other European countries, is the result of a huge effort by a few key people. Their aim was always to provide a symbol to commemorate those killed in the First World War. This was the 'Great War', the 'war to end all wars', and the tribute was both for the enormous numbers killed and for the terrible conditions that were endured by all.

The total number of casualties can be assessed in many different ways. It depends on whether you include only deaths on the battlefields or those who died later of war wounds, physical and psychological; whether you include the genocides (disputed by Turkey) of the Armenians and Greeks in the Ottoman Empire; whether you include deaths that resulted directly from malnutrition caused by the war, and so on. Even just including the deaths in combat, the number comes to around 6.8 million; from other associated sources the number probably exceeds fifteen million. Official figures from around 1920 for the UK and its colonies at the time were approximately 830,000 for those killed in combat. For the installation of poppies in London in 2014 the figure they used was 888,246. If you include the dead, wounded or missing, the figure rises to nearly three million for the UK and its colonies.[1]

When thinking of casualties we have to consider the famous 'Spanish flu' epidemic that raged immediately after the war as well. This killed another 200,000 people in Britain and up to fifty million worldwide.[2] It spread to the remotest corners of the world and killed a staggering 3 to 5 per cent of the world's population at the time, making it the gravest epidemic since the Black Death. As an influenza it was unusual; it killed mainly young adults, because of an overreaction of their immune systems, while children and the elderly were better able to survive. The initial mutation that caused the deadly outbreak, which appeared in the summer of 1918, is thought to have been triggered by the trench war, probably in France or possibly even in Kansas or the Far East, but almost certainly not in Spain. It was reported in more detail from Spain, mainly, it seems, because the Spanish were *not* directly involved in the war, hence 'Spanish flu'.

The scale of the casualties of the war was unprecedented, as was the effect on survivors. Previous wars had involved far fewer people; this one had involved nearly everyone in Britain, and in many other European countries in some form, so all were aware of the sheer horror that had been unleashed. That led to much more serious questioning about the fundamental causes of war than had ever happened before. What indeed had this war actually achieved? It was this deep sense of shock and tragedy that led to the huge change in attitude towards war, towards empire and everything they represented. One thing was agreed by everyone: nothing like this must ever happen again. Such a tragedy needed a symbol. The poppy emerged as the symbol as it had emerged on the battlefields, as a resonant image of the soldiers' blood.[3]

Almost immediately, selling poppies became a way of raising money for returning soldiers and their families. The proceeds went to widows, orphans and surviving ex-servicemen, especially the injured. Gradually people realized that many of the surviving soldiers that returned still able-bodied had serious problems returning to civilian life. They were often traumatized, some seriously. This was very little understood and mostly ignored. We have become far more aware of these problems in recent years and any money raised from poppy selling is now used to help ex-servicemen and women in any way they need it.

As we know only too well, the 'war to end all wars' did no such thing, and the poppy became the symbol of fallen soldiers in the Second World War too. Subsequent European wars have been smaller in scale, though devastating to particular communities. The poppy has become the universal symbol to commemorate all of these, and remains open as a symbol for all future casualties in conflict. The simplicity of the symbol has meant that the poppy can include any and all associations that anyone makes with wars.

## How the Poppy Became the Symbol

The dead, especially of the First World War, are frequently referred to as 'the fallen'. This appellation comes from Laurence Binyon's poem 'For the Fallen', published in *The Times* in September 1914, only a month after Britain had joined the war. The fourth stanza (of seven), which Binyon said had come to him first, is the one quoted at every Remembrance Sunday ceremony:

They shall not grow old as we that are left grow old:
Age shall not weary them, nor the years condemn.
At the going down of the sun and in the morning
We will remember them.

From the start of trench warfare there were terrible losses on both sides, and conditions quickly deteriorated amid the shelling in the wet mud and churned-up soil. The dead were frequently left unburied, at least for some time, and many graves were dug on the battlefields.

It is interesting to note here that the first 'Remembrance Day' was actually held on 4 August 1915, the first anniversary of the declaration of war in Britain. No poppies were involved at that stage. Although commemorating the casualties, it mainly acted to recruit more people to the army, and the crowd declared itself determined to 'continue to a victorious end'. By 1918 the tone was very different, the Remembrance Day 'silently paying tribute to the Empire's sons who have fallen on the scattered battlefields of the world war'.[4]

The trenches and mass movement of people, the constant shelling and digging of graves turned battlefields into huge expanses of bare mud through the winters. It was these conditions that led, in 1915, to the growth and flowering of poppies in profusion all around the graves and on the battlefields, where they had not been seen the previous year. It must have seemed a miraculous commemoration of the dead soldiers; both the digging and the shells had provided conditions similar to ploughing. It took another poem, 'In Flanders Fields', published anonymously by *Punch* on 8 December 1915, to create the association of the fallen soldiers with poppies:

> In Flanders fields the poppies blow
> Between the crosses, row on row,
> That mark our place; and in the sky
> The larks, still bravely singing, fly
> Scarce heard amid the guns below.
>
> We are the Dead. Short days ago
> We lived, felt dawn, saw sunset glow,
> Loved and were loved, and now we lie
> In Flanders fields.
>
> Take up our quarrel with the foe:
> To you from failing hands we throw

The torch; be yours to hold it high.
If ye break faith with us who die
We shall not sleep, though poppies grow
In Flanders fields.

It turned out that this poem was written by Lieutenant-Colonel John McCrae, a Canadian medical officer, born in 1873, who had served on the Western Front in 1914 and had been in charge of a field hospital at the Second Battle of Ypres in 1915. The death of his student and friend Alexis Helmer probably inspired the poem. He wrote it quickly, on 3 May 1915, and his companions immediately recognized its heartfelt content, and how well it summed up what had been going on. McCrae then actually discarded his poem and it took a fellow officer to rescue it and send it to several potential publishers in London, including *Punch*, which is why it was published anonymously. Many people had seen the poppies in abundance on the battlefields and the red colour aptly matched the bloodshed. It therefore became the perfect symbol. The poem was almost immediately picked up and published and read across the world. *Punch* included McCrae's name in the index to that year, so his fame was assured.

This one poem did not, by itself, turn the poppy into the international symbol it became. It took an American teacher, Moina Belle Michael, at the end of the war to champion the cause. Moina Michael had toured Europe in the summer of 1914 and had been in Germany shortly after Archduke Franz Ferdinand was assassinated in Sarajevo. Along with many other Americans in Europe at the time, she made her way quickly to Italy to avoid the rapidly spreading conflicts (Germany declared war on Russia on 1 August) and find a boat back to America.

America finally entered the war in 1917. Moina Michael wanted to enlist but the only way she could do so at her age, 47, was to apply for war work with the YMCA. While working with the YMCA as an overseas war secretary she attended a conference at Columbia University in New York, two days before the armistice, in November 1918. The story, recalled in her autobiography, is that when the other 24 delegates at the conference were occupied elsewhere she picked up a copy of the latest issue of the *Ladies' Home Journal* in which the surgical suppliers Bauer and Black had placed a patriotic advertisement.[5] This included a copy of McCrae's famous poem (retitled 'We Shall Not Sleep') and, alongside it, Philip Lyford's vivid colour illustration of a cemetery and fire with dead soldiers, or 'doughboys' as they were known then in America, and poppies around the base.

Although Moina Michael knew the poem already, seeing it with the picture motivated her: 'In a high moment of white resolve I pledged to KEEP THE FAITH and always to wear a red poppy of Flanders Fields as a sign of remembrance and the emblem of "keeping the faith with all who died".' When the conference members returned and she mentioned her pledge to them, they were all taken by the idea, probably influenced strongly by Michael's enthusiasm for it, and requested poppies to wear as a symbol of remembrance. Between them they gave her $10 to buy some and she had to go and find some suitable poppies straight away. This, naturally, was not altogether easy – people did not have artificial poppies in the way they do now. She ran around the shops of New York trying to find poppies and was just about to give up when she entered Wanamaker's store and there were some silk poppies. She bought these and when she returned to the conference room she gave one to each of the delegates. The tradition of poppies worn in lapels for remembrance had started. Soon after this she wrote her own poem, 'We Shall Keep the Faith':

> Oh! you who sleep in Flanders Fields,
> Sleep sweet – to rise anew!
> We caught the torch you threw
> And holding high, we keep the Faith
> With All who died.

Advertisement that inspired a symbol: Bauer and Black's advertisement for surgical supplies, using a painting by Philip Lyford that inspired Moina Michael.

We cherish, too, the poppy red
That grows on fields where valor led;
It seems to signal to the skies
That blood of heroes never dies,
But lends a luster to the red
Of the flower that blooms above the dead
In Flanders Fields.

And now the Torch and Poppy Red
We wear in honor of our dead.
Fear not that ye have died for naught;
We'll teach the lesson that ye wrought
In Flanders Fields.

With this poem she had caught the spirit of the times, though she never claimed any great literary merit. She then campaigned hard to get the poppy recognized as the universal symbol of remembrance. She realized quickly that it would double as the perfect symbol to raise awareness of the plight of returning war veterans and of the bereaved families, and could be used to raise money for them. Though many people liked her idea, it still did not take off immediately. One boost to the association came with a poster of 1918, designed by the artist Frank Lucien Nicolet, born in Sussex of English and French parents but brought up in Canada. This was one, and probably the most effective, of several that bore the slogan 'Buy Victory Bonds', the Canadian equivalent of the British War Loans. These were designed to appeal to people's patriotic sense to finance the war and perhaps to control inflation.

The poppy symbol is potent, largely because it is so simple. There was an attempt to make the symbol a much bigger and more complicated one with a 'Flanders Victory Memorial Flag', designed with flags of the Allies and the American Liberty torch as well as poppies. This failed, probably as a result of being too complicated and giving mixed messages about victory, Allied resistance and remembrance of the dead all at once.

'Buy Victory Bonds': Frank Lucien Nicolet's propaganda poster, 1918.

Moina Michael rather lost heart again after the flag had failed to catch people's imaginations, and felt that her efforts had been in vain, until she heard that returning soldiers were being greeted by cafés and bars decked out with artificial poppies. In some places customers were taking the poppies in return for a donation, to pin to their clothing so that they could demonstrate solidarity with the returning soldiers. Once she had got wind of this she attended her local branch of the American Legion in Georgia in August 1920 and again put forward her idea with vigour. She convinced them of the potency of the symbol and they promised to take it to the National Convention of the legion that was meeting in Ohio in September. To Michael's delight, the American Legion took it up and it became their symbol.

Once America had taken up the idea the rest of the Allied countries followed quickly. Canada took it up in the summer of 1921 and Michael then presented the idea to Field Marshal Earl Haig in Britain, the founder and president of the British Legion. In November 1921 he adopted it as the symbol of the British Legion too and launched the first Poppy Day appeal. The poppy symbol was shortly afterwards adopted by Australia and New Zealand as well.

POPPY

Meanwhile one more person became a vital part of the spread. The idea of using artificially made poppies for sale as remembrance symbols had been taken up by a young Frenchwoman, Anna Guérin. She had attended the American Legion convention and saw the potential in the idea. When she returned to France she encouraged bereaved women and their families, then very poor and suffering terribly from the consequences of the war, to make paper and silk poppies for sale to America and Britain. They made millions of them, and between 1920 and 1924 most poppies were made in France. Seeing the success of Guérin's venture and the potential for the British market, Haig set up a British Legion factory in England in 1922. He employed disabled war veterans, and by 1924 they were making 27 million poppies each year. By 1926 the factory was moved to an old brewery in Richmond and then to a new purpose-built factory in 1932.[6] This still runs today, and currently it supplies 36 million poppies each year.

At the suggestion of Haig's wife, a second factory was set up in Edinburgh in 1926, and it is now known as 'Lady Haig's Factory', though since 2011 the two factories have become part of a single charity. The Scottish factory currently produces a further five million poppies per year. It makes paper poppies to a slightly different design from the English one, using four paper lobes for the petals rather than the standard design of two 'petals' for the English poppy. The real poppy has flowers with four petals, formed from two whorls of two petals, so the Scottish design is closer to the wild plant. Other people have, inevitably, made other poppy designs; there are even some designed with five petals, which really is wrong. Many flowers do have five petals and it is so much more common generally than four that we perhaps think of the five-petalled flower as a kind of 'perfect', basic flower. But poppies never have five petals, except if there has been a peculiarity in the development of the flower, and then the petals will not be evenly spaced. In Canada the poppies are made of plastic with a flocked surface, generally with four petals.

Royal British Legion poppies.

Anna Guérin's intervention was, in a way, rather strange. French soldiers in the First World War wore a uniform with the colour known as 'horizon blue', a pastel greyish blue. Earlier uniforms were red, and this marked a change to a more camouflaged colour at the same time as the British and others started wearing khaki. The soldiers became known as 'Les Bleuets' – 'The Blues' or 'The Bluets' – and the association emerged between soldiers and the colour blue. The colour used for the uniform derived as a dye from the leaves of the woad plant, long known to produce a bluish dye and grown for that purpose, particularly in Picardie. But the woad flower is actually yellow and so was not a suitable symbol. 'Le bleuet' is the French name for the cornflower, *Centaurea cyanus*. This has an intense blue colour and, like the poppy, is a cornfield weed and came up on the battlefields after all the disturbance caused to the soil. It is now rare in Britain, though still common in parts of France. So the poppy was not taken up as the remembrance symbol in France; it was the bleuet that became the symbol for France's fallen soldiers.

Moina Michael died in 1944, by which time she had raised more than $200 million for war veterans. She was well known in America and had been dubbed 'The Poppy Lady'. One posthumous accolade she received was in 1948 when the USA printed a three-cent postage stamp depicting her with a poppy. Her light may have dimmed a bit in recent years, but without her we would not have today's universally recognized symbol.

McCrae's poem inspired his fellow Canadian poet Edna Jaques to write another rather similar poem, called simply 'Flanders Now', beginning: 'We have kept faith, ye Flanders' dead, Sleep well beneath those poppies red'. This was first published in the *Calgary Herald* in 1921 but taken up by various papers and eventually published, alongside the Belgian national anthem, in cards of Everywoman's Club which was raising money for a library in Brussels. It helped to raise

French soldiers from 1916 in their 'horizon blue' uniform.

Cornflowers, 'Les Bleuets', in southern France.

U.S.$1 million, although Jaques did not receive any financial benefit herself. It was also read at the unveiling of the Tomb of the Unknown Soldier in Washington, DC, on Armistice Day 1921.

Any other poet writing about the war will have been aware of John McCrae's poem, because it became so well known. One of the best known of the British war poets is Isaac Rosenberg. He never had the patriotic zeal for the war shared by many of his contemporaries, and felt its futility and its dreadful toll from the beginning. His poetry has a much more resigned feel to it than McCrae's. Paul Fussell, in his study of war literature, regarded the following poem, published in December 1916, as perhaps the greatest poem ever to come out of the First World War.[7] Rosenberg made the explicit association of the poppies with the blood of fallen soldiers in his poem 'Break of Day in the Trenches':

> The darkness crumbles away.
> It is the same old druid Time as ever,
> Only a live thing leaps my hand,
> A queer sardonic rat,
> As I pull the parapet's poppy

To stick behind my ear.
Droll rat, they would shoot you if they knew
Your cosmopolitan sympathies.
Now you have touched this English hand
You will do the same to a German
Soon, no doubt, if it be your pleasure
To cross the sleeping green between.
It seems you inwardly grin as you pass
Strong eyes, fine limbs, haughty athletes,
Less chanced than you for life,
Bonds to the whims of murder,
Sprawled in the bowels of the earth,
The torn fields of France.
What do you see in our eyes
At the shrieking iron and flame
Hurled through still heavens?
What quaver – what heart aghast?
Poppies whose roots are in man's veins
Drop, and are ever dropping;
But mine in my ear is safe –
Just a little white with the dust.

One of Britain's official artists of the First World War was Sir William Orpen. He visited the battlefields of the Somme in summer 1917 following the famous offensive that occurred between July and November the previous year. He described how he had seen the Somme that winter as a morass of desolate shell-holes, water and mud, but that following summer,

no words could express the beauty of it. The dreary, dismal mud was baked white and pure – dazzling white. Red poppies, and a blue flower, great masses of them, stretched for miles and miles. The sky was a pure dark blue, and the whole air, up to a height of about forty feet, thick with

U.S. three-cent stamp of 1948, with Moina Michael and her poppies.

white butterflies. It was like an enchanted land; but in the place of faeries, there were thousands of little white crosses, marked Unknown British Soldier.[8]

Orpen's 'blue flower' was almost certainly the bleuet, the cornflower, taken up as a remembrance symbol by France for the very reason Orpen mentions it. It is interesting that he clearly did not recognize what it was; perhaps it was rare in Britain even by the First World War. He appears not to have left a painting of this scene, sadly, despite the vivid description.

There have been many poems since the First World War commemorating the fallen, often citing poppies, and some, like Michael's and Jaques's, quoting McCrae. More were written after the Second World War, prominent among these being Vernon Scannell's deeply moving 'The Great War' (1962), which includes the lines:

> Whenever the November sky
> Quivers with a bugle's hoarse, sweet cry,
> The reason darkens; in its evening gleam
> Crosses and flares, tormented wire, grey earth,
> Splattered with crimson flowers . . .

The poppy has become the symbol of remembrance of those who have died in war in so many countries that it is recognized almost universally. Millions of poppies made of paper or other materials are sold in November to commemorate the armistice, celebrated on Remembrance Sunday, the second Sunday of November – the nearest Sunday to the eleventh hour of the eleventh day of the eleventh month, the date and time that the armistice was signed in 1918. Now the British Legion has a travel company, Remembrance Travel, and in 2007 they started calling themselves, unofficially at least, 'Poppy Travel' for their 'battlefield tours'.[9]

All wars since the 'Great War' are usually included in remembrance celebrations, most obviously the Second World War. The poppy's popularity has grown over the years, and the remembrance ceremonies in Britain have kept up to date with the inclusion of all the later wars, such as the Falklands in 1982, and the twenty-first-century wars in Iraq and Afghanistan.

## Some Ramifications of the Poppy Symbol

At times the ceremonies surrounding 'Poppy Day' have looked as if they are glorifying war. This must be partly because McCrae's poem does include an urge for people to fight on in remembrance of the dead. His poem, we must remember, was written within a year of the start of the war, in May 1915, and there was plenty of fighting still to come. It was mainly a few years after the war that people really started to feel the futility of the whole conflict, and the fact that so many had died with little or no gain for anyone.

In the first few years after the First World War, the celebrations became particularly jingoistic, and stirred up some resentful feelings in many people. A big celebration in the Royal Albert Hall included a *World Requiem*, written specially by John Foulds.[10] This featured massed soloists, choirs including off-stage choirs, organ and full symphony orchestra. The first performance, in 1923, involved 1,250 musicians. It was performed again in 1924 and 1926. In the early 1920s the celebrations included some victory balls and dinners. It was the fact that these celebrations seemed to be glorifying war that led to the widespread change of heart. This change was particularly brought about by a prominent early peace campaigner, Canon Dick Sheppard of London's St Martin-in-the-Fields. He wrote a letter to

*The Times* in October 1925 complaining that a victory ball to be held in the Albert Hall on the Saturday evening before Remembrance Sunday was totally inappropriate, and that the day and the poppy symbol should represent the fallen soldiers and not be a celebration of war. He was an outspoken pacifist and attracted a large following for his sermons and writings. As a result of his actions, and the huge popular support he had, rather surprisingly the Royal Albert Hall did immediately delay the ball, even if only by a day, and replaced it with a more solemn event. The following year this report appeared in the *Daily Express*:

> The really astonishing feature of Armistice Day this
> year was its pronounced seriousness. As time passes
> the sense of jubilation on this day of memory decreases.
> There was a marked difference, even from last year . . .
> There were many dances then, and the restaurants and
> night clubs were full to overflowing. Many people who
> danced last Armistice Day felt that they could not do
> so last night.[11]

Sheppard had had a profound effect on the national mood. He issued a nationwide call for 'peace pledges' in 1934, and eventually formed the Peace Pledge Union.[12] This was given its formal constitution in 1936, the year before he died. Vera Brittain, best known for her moving account of the casualties of the First World War, *Testament of Youth*, based her character of the Revd Robert Carbury, in her novel *Born 1925*, on Canon Sheppard.[13] The Peace Pledge Union is the oldest 'secular' organization specifically campaigning for an end to all wars. In its current publicity material it specifically condemns most, if not all, Remembrance Day celebrations as jingoistic glorification of the military and of war generally. It has nearly as strong words for the British and Commonwealth war cemeteries, of which there are around 23,000 in 148 countries around the world. They see the educational trips that visit these, and other commemorations

Poppy petals descending at the climax of the annual Remembrance Day
ceremony in the Royal Albert Hall, 2014.

of war, as recruiters of young people to the military. They point out that war is big business and selling arms plays a major role in world politics. The explicit aim of the Peace Pledge Union is to counter all such potential celebrations, give conscientious objectors their due, and publicize 'peace memorials' instead of war memorials.

In 1927 Remembrance Day celebrations had changed into a 'Festival of Remembrance' that has continued to this day in the Royal Albert Hall every November. This includes military displays, but also music and prayers for the fallen. At the culmination of the festival, thousands of poppy petals are released from the roof of the hall. Currently there are two ceremonies, an afternoon one open to the public and an evening one for members of the British Legion and royalty. Foulds's requiem was forgotten after 1926 but was revived for the 2007 festival and then recorded. The Festival of Remembrance was suspended in 1939 because of the start of the Second World War, but resumed in subsequent years.

Since Canon Sheppard's early campaign there have been many other protests by peace campaigners about the wearing of poppies. There are, or were, those veterans who could never forgive Haig for how they were led in the First World War, and so would never wear the symbol that he championed.

As early as 1933 the Women's Cooperative Guild (or Cooperative Women's Guild) decided to wear a white poppy as a pacifist protest. A few women even lost their jobs over wearing it because their employers felt that they were being disrespectful to the dead. White poppies are now sold by the Peace Pledge Union with the statement: 'War is a crime against humanity. I renounce war and am therefore determined not to support any kind of war. I am also determined to work for the removal of all causes of war.'[14] The Society of Friends, or Quakers, a famously pacifist society, have encouraged their members to wear a white poppy alongside a red one, and in so doing, both commemorate the fallen and campaign for an end to all war at the same time.

In 2006 yet another poppy colour appeared, this time a purple one. This was issued by Animal Aid, to commemorate the animals

that lost their lives in war service.[15] Animal Aid have stated: 'During human conflicts, animals have been used as messengers, for detection, scouting and rescue, as beasts of burden and on the frontline. Please wear a purple poppy and help us raise awareness of these forgotten victims.' The British Legion has accepted both white and purple poppies as part of the Remembrance Day celebrations, suggesting that people wear them alongside the traditional red poppy. They simply suggest that sellers should not offer two colours together as this could be confusing.

Recently, with fewer and fewer Europeans remembering what it is like to fight on their own or nearby soil, there have been the inevitable arguments about the rights and wrongs of wearing poppies in particular situations. There is little doubt that the potency of the symbol is waning as the two twentieth-century world wars fade into history. In places people have been dubbed 'poppy fascists' when there is a genuine or perceived insistence on wearing a poppy in early November at all times or risk being ostracized from a group. One trenchant article about this was published on 7 November 2013 in *The Independent*. Robert Fisk, well known for his controversial views, wrote an article entitled 'Poppycock – or Why Remembrance Rituals Make Me See Red: The Poppy Helps Us Avoid a Search for the Meaning of War'. He refers to the poppy as 'an obscene fashion appendage, inspired by a pro-war poem'.[16] His contention is that those who wear a poppy come close to glorifying war. His father, who had fought on the Somme, was one of those veterans who refused to wear one after reading a biography of Earl Haig, whom he regarded as responsible for the loss of life in such a senseless war. Others have refused to wear one as they see it as political justification for continuing wars, especially the most recent 'War on Terror' and conflicts in the Middle East. Many other articles have been written on both sides and this led Dan Hodges of the *Daily Telegraph* to suggest that there is always a 'war of the poppy' every Remembrance Day.[17]

Remembrance Day has taken on particular political significance on occasion. The most poignant example must be that of Northern Ireland. Ever since the partition of Ireland in 1920–22, there has been simmering, and often overt, sectarian violence between the majority Protestant and minority Catholic communities in Northern Ireland. The poppy became strongly, and as it turned out disastrously, associated with the Protestant cause almost from its inception as a symbol. What seems to have sealed the association was the use of the symbol by a Protestant paramilitary group, the Ulster Volunteer Force. They erected murals to commemorate their murdered comrades, illustrated with poppies. This Ulster division had been in the vanguard of fighting at the Battle of the Somme in 1916 and many were killed, but the association was clearly made with Protestant unionists. The poppy became a Protestant symbol, and therefore a symbol of oppression.

The Catholic Republican community had formed the political party Sinn Fein, with its underground military wing, the Provisional Irish Republican Army (IRA). The aim of the IRA was to target the military side of the Protestant community. Inevitably, with the poppy symbol taking on its sectarian significance, a Remembrance Day parade became an appropriate target – poppies everywhere symbolizing, as they saw it, Protestant power, and a large contingent of military personnel all parading together. In 1987, Remembrance Day, Sunday 8 November, saw one of the worst atrocities of the conflict, known as the 'Poppy Day massacre'. A bomb that had been planted by the IRA exploded at 10.43 am in the small Northern Ireland town of Enniskillen in County Fermanagh. It had been placed in the reading room of the town and blew out its walls against which many people were standing. Eleven people were killed outright and a twelfth died later of injuries, all but one of whom were civilians. All were Protestants. A further 63 were injured. The IRA said later that they were aiming to kill members of the Ulster Defence Regiment, who were parading for the ceremony.

There was widespread revulsion against the killing on both sides of the sectarian divide, and the outrage caused by this bombing was much wider because of the timing on such a solemn occasion. One aspect that is particularly remembered is the reaction of Gordon

Mural in Northern Ireland commemorating Protestant paramilitary group the Ulster Volunteer Force.

Wilson, whose daughter, Marie, was killed by the blast. In his speech immediately afterwards, broadcast around the world, he said that he did not bear ill will or grudge against the bombers however much he missed his daughter. The killings were condemned not only within Ireland and Britain, but by some of the IRA's sponsors, including Colonel Gaddafi of Libya, who stopped supplying arms to them. The Remembrance Day service in Enniskillen was restaged two weeks later with around 7,000 people attending, Catholic and Protestant, and including Margaret Thatcher, the British prime minister. The incident led to a rapid decline in support for the IRA. Ten years later the Sinn Fein president, Gerry Adams, apologized for the killings. The IRA admitted that it had actually planted another, larger, bomb in the village of Tullyhommon some 20 miles away that they intended should explode at around the same time as the Enniskillen bomb. It had failed to detonate. This was then defused.

There remains in Ireland a deep ambivalence over the significance of the poppy symbol. Whatever is said or known about it as a remembrance symbol for all who have died in wars, it is still seen by many as Protestant and, to the Catholic population, a symbol of oppression.

Michael Longley, a Belfast poet, some years later, and surely in the light of the extra political symbolism in Northern Ireland, could write a poem, 'Poppies', that gives a very different feel to the meaning of the symbol from those of the war poets:

I

Some people tried to stop other people wearing poppies
And ripped them from lapels as though uprooting poppies
From Flanders fields, but the others hid inside their
    poppies
Razor blades and added to their poppies more red poppies.

II

In Royal Avenue they tossed in the air with so much joy
Returning wounded soldiers, their stitches burst for joy.[18]

The poppy symbol remains very much alive in Canada. Here between 2001 and 2005 the ten-dollar note was printed with a war memorial, poppies and McCrae's poem on the reverse. With McCrae they are clearly honouring their own. The bill was withdrawn in 2013 in favour of a railway design. In 2004 two commemorative 'quarters' (25 cents) were produced – silver coins, with one or two red poppies painted on them.

## War Memorials

War memorials for Allied soldiers are often decked with poppy wreaths throughout the year, and all have them on Remembrance Sunday. The poppy symbol has become just as much part of the Second World War memorials as it has for the First World War. Poppy wreaths appear in Normandy to commemorate the D-Day landings, as at the so-called Pegasus Bridge over the river Orne at Ouistreham near Caen. This was the very first landing of all the invading Allied troops, just after midnight on 6 June 1944. Paratroopers, with a Pegasus logo, giving the bridge its nickname, arrived in gliders under the command of Major John Howard and quickly took over the bridge. A plaque commemorates the casualties of this landing. Major Howard's grave in the village of Clifton Hampden in Oxfordshire is surrounded by a wreath of similar artificial poppies in tribute to him.

There are numerous memorials, large and small, across Britain and usually there is at least one artificial poppy, and often several, or a wreath, around each one. One of the most touching is a small memorial next to the South Downs way in West Sussex, on the hill above Didling. It is to 'Hauptmann Joseph Oestermann', a German pilot shot down on the first day of the Battle of Britain on 13 August 1940. He was on a bombing raid to Britain, so was an enemy, but the memorial stone is clearly well tended to this day and, naturally, decorated with artificial poppies. He was German but a young man, only 25 years old, and killed in action just like so many sons.

Memorial of the allied attack at Ouistreham, D-Day 1944, beside the Pegasus Bridge. Note the Pegasus logo on the stone.

Major Howard's grave, Clifton Hampden.

Memorial to 'Hauptmann Joseph Oestermann', South Downs, Sussex.

In 1995, fifty years after the end of the Second World War, stained glass depicting poppies was inserted as the west window into the small village church at Noke in Oxfordshire. The memorial plaque below the window cites the two losses from this tiny village, one in 1915 and one in 1944.

The Royal Mail issued commemorative postage stamps on 6 November 2008 in time for Remembrance Day that year, the ninetieth anniversary of the armistice. They put together three stylized poppy stamps, two of which had been issued in the two previous years. These incorporated a barbed-wire stem in one, and depictions of soldiers in the other two as part of the flower. A further poppy stamp was issued on 28 July 2014 as part of a series to commemorate the start of the First World War. This was designed by Fiona Strickland and, perhaps a little unfortunately, depicted a 'double' poppy, a cultivated form rather than a wild one. Yet another poppy stamp was issued in a series of symbolic flowers on 17 September 2014, designed by the botanical artist Kate Stephens. There have been other poppy stamps, such as a set of six stylized stamps including war features issued by Jersey in 2014 and earlier stamps from Poland, Andorra and the USA.

In 2014 commemorations of the start of the First World War dominated headlines in all media outlets. Poppies featured prominently in a number of them. In one initiative, backed by a Heritage Lottery Fund grant of £100,000, the British prime minister, David Cameron, launched an appeal to schoolchildren to plant real poppies to mark the centenary of the outbreak of the First World War. If planted then (in April) or soon after, the idea was that they would be in flower by 4 August, the date war broke out in 1914.

Several writers have commemorated the start of the First World War either as history or in novel form. Examples are Mary Hooper, a popular writer of historical romances, who published *Poppy* in 2014 and followed this up with *Poppy in the Field* (2015), both about the First

Stained-glass window with poppies at Noke St Giles church,
Oxfordshire, inserted in 1995.

Double poppy on
Royal Mail stamp.

Poppy, F Strickland

World War. The teenage heroine is the 'Poppy' of the titles, but the association with the symbol is clear and the cover illustrations include war scenes with poppies. Hilary Robinson and Martin Impey published a short picture book called *Where the Poppies Now Grow*, designed as a graphic novel for children and adults. There are many others.

The most ambitious commemoration of the First World War has been the immense installation of ceramic poppies in the dry moat surrounding the Tower of London. This display was the brainchild of ceramic artist Paul Cummins, and was staged by theatre designer Tom Piper. The installation was named *Blood Swept Lands and Seas of Red*, after a line from a poem in the will that Cummins discovered of a Derbyshire man who was killed in Flanders. The first ceramic poppy was 'planted' on 17 July 2014 and the incomplete installation was unveiled on the anniversary of the outbreak of Britain's declaration of war on 5 August 2014. There was a general invitation to sponsor a poppy at £25 each, and the sponsor would receive the poppy once the installation had been taken down. The installation received extensive coverage across the country and beyond. It captured the public imagination and numerous volunteers helped plant the poppies. All the poppies were eventually sponsored. A Roll of Honour was instigated, and 180 names of casualties in the Great War were read out each evening between Monday 11 August and Monday 10 November, followed by the Last Post. The complete installation of 888,246 ceramic poppies was all in place by Armistice Day, 11 November 2014. The number chosen was one of the most recent estimates of direct First World War casualties from Britain and its then colonies. The Tower was surrounded by poppies – indeed a sea of red from a distance. They included two large metalwork structures rising above the moat, known as the 'Weeping Window' and the 'Wave'. The 'Weeping Window' spilled out from a window about 6 metres from the ground and the 'Wave' formed an arch over the entrance to the Tower. In these, the stems of the poppies were contorted and tangled together. They could be interpreted in several ways – perhaps the waves of soldiers going over the sides of the trenches, nearly always to their certain death, and the barbed wire in the trenches. These symbolic forms and the entire scale of the installation gave a vivid demonstration of the catastrophic loss of life in the conflict.

For the basic poppy design, Paul Cummins chose to depict six petals in two whorls of three. Poppies have four petals, although some members of the family have six, but he saw that some Canadian designs had six and the symbol was, after all, inspired by a Canadian poet. Cummins felt that it was a design that lent itself particularly well to the poppies in his installation and the six petals also reflected the six service charities that were to benefit from the installation.[19] Cummins's poppies are about 8 cm (3 in.) across the petals, but each poppy was individually sculpted. Any profits from the sponsorship have been given to charity, and the British Legion and other military-based charities have benefited by more than £15 million. Dismantling of the installation started immediately after Armistice Day, 2014, at the artist's instruction, and it was all gone by the end of November. This was to emphasize the transience of life. An estimated five million people visited the Tower to see it during its brief showing between August and November 2014. The aftermath perhaps gave a different, unintentionally vivid, remembrance of the war, as the moat inevitably had much of its grass scraped away and looked like a muddy and desolate trench.

Lady Susie Sainsbury's Backstage Trust has now bought the 'Weeping Window', and the Clore Duffield Foundation has bought

Part of Paul Cummins's installation of 888,246 ceramic
poppies at the Tower of London in 2014.

the 'Wave', with help from government money. These will go on tour
to several sites across Britain between 2015 and 2018 and will then
be on permanent display at the Imperial War Museums in London
and Manchester as part of the NOW legacy projects, responsible for
First World War centenary art commissions.

We think of the poppy as being intrinsically European, and the
symbol a British one – after all, the plant is a very long-established
feature through much of Europe including Britain, and the war was
fought in northern Europe. It is curious to think that the poem that
inspired it was written by a Canadian, the symbolism championed

A section of Paul Cummins's installation before it was completed, showing the 'Wave'
of poppies cascading over the tower's entrance.

by an American and the first legion to adopt the symbol was that of the USA. Even the first mass production of poppies was the idea of a Frenchwoman, in a country that adopted the cornflower as its symbol and not the poppy.

The latest idea is for the formation of a 'Virtual Poppy Field', a website designed to commemorate all of the dead. You can enter the name of someone you wish to commemorate or have someone allocated to you and upload a picture.[20]

There have been calls for the commemorations to include all those killed in the First World War, not just those on the British side.

## Earlier Associations with War

The poppy had been noticed on battlefields before the First World War, and one of the reasons it was picked up so enthusiastically was because the association already existed. The earliest reference must be that in Homer's *Iliad*, where King Priam of Troy's son, Gorgythio(n), said to be both beautiful and blameless, is killed by an arrow intended for his brother, Hector:

> the weapon flies
> At Hector's breast, and sings along the skies:
> He miss'd the mark; but pierced Gorgythio's heart,
> And drench'd in royal blood the thirsty dart.
> (Fair Castianira, nymph of form divine,
> This offspring added to king Priam's line.)
> As full-blown poppies, overcharged with rain,
> Decline the head, and drooping kiss the plain;
> So sinks the youth: his beauteous head, depress'd
> Beneath his helmet, drops upon his breast.
> (translation by Alexander Pope, 1720)

Although this poppy is merely a simile rather than any form of commemoration of the dead, the association with blood is surely present. Homer's allusion to poppies was picked up by Virgil in the *Aeneid* and, in the sixteenth century, by the Italian poet Ariosto, giving rise to the idea of 'tall poppies'.

It is recorded that the hills and valleys that were to stage the Battle of Waterloo, fought in 1815 exactly one hundred years before McCrae's poem, made a contented scene decked with hundreds of poppies, but that the grass would soon be stained by blood as crimson as the poppies. After the battle, the fields were ploughed and the poppies that emerged were said to have sprung from the blood of the dead soldiers. Some said that the poppies were mocking the dead soldiers with their blood-red blooms.[21]

In some autobiographical notes, John Clare, born in 1793, mentions making 'Cockades etc. of corn poppies and bluebottles [cornflowers]' as a child.[22] Perhaps military headgear was already associated with these two plants by the early nineteenth century, and it is fitting that Clare includes what were to become both the British and the French emblems.

The historian Lord Macaulay wrote in 1855 about the Battle of Landen in 1693, part of the Nine Years War. Landen is very close to the First World War battlefield at Ypres. Macaulay's description of the site associates the poppy with death and destruction:

> The next summer the soil, fertilized by twenty thousand
> corpses, broke forth into millions of poppies. The traveller
> who, on the road from Saint Tron to Tirlemont, saw
> that vast sheet of rich scarlet spreading from Landen
> to Neerwinden, could hardly help fancying that the
> figurative prediction of the Hebrew prophet was literally
> accomplished, that the earth was disclosing her blood,
> and refusing to cover the slain.[23]

Macaulay may well have been exaggerating, and his sources may not be entirely accurate, but the association was clearly strong by the time he wrote this passage. The Hebrew prophet in question is Isaiah: 'For behold the Lord cometh out of his place to punish the inhabitants of the earth for their iniquity: the earth also shall disclose her blood, and shall no more cover her slain' (Isaiah 26:21).

The American poet, critic and travel writer Bayard Taylor, in his travels through Syria, Lebanon and other nearby places in the 1850s, mentions the abundance of poppies several times: 'The old battlefields of Syria, densely covered with blood-red poppies, blooming in barbaric splendour, gloating on the gore of soldiers slain.'[24] It is possible, in this part of the world, that the poppies were other species, but even here they are likely to have been the corn poppy.

The poppy symbol, then, had some strong precedents, especially from the nineteenth century, and perhaps we can say that the association of poppies and war dead was in the cultural background of Europe before the First World War. It is undoubtedly here to stay, and, for most of us, remains a powerful reminder of both the fallen soldiers and the cost that was paid in lives for many of the freedoms that we enjoy today.

seven

# Opium

꧁꧂

Poppies produce opium. In so doing, they have been the unwitting perpetrators of a huge influence on human behaviour, both positive and negative. Plants that produce drugs, or other unnecessary but desirable substances such as spices, have influenced human history more than most food plants. Columbus was seeking spices when he made his famous voyage. Coffee, tea and tobacco have been classic slave crops and the narcotic effects of various plants, including coca, cannabis and opium, have been used in rituals for millennia. The potent substances occur in a small quantity within the plants, and most of the plants grow in the tropics or subtropics. The difficulties of finding them, or of collecting and distributing them, have given many drugs an exotic air, at least until recently. The combination of being hard to obtain and highly desirable is a powerful mix and, as a result, most spices and drugs have been expensive. The illegal status of many of the drugs, though intermittent until the twentieth and twenty-first centuries in most countries in the West, has only added to their appeal in certain sections of society.

The effects of drugs can be magical on the nervous system in the early stages of use and almost all, including opium, are highly addictive, so people are prepared to go to great lengths and considerable expense to obtain them. As is well known, regular use means that a steadily greater quantity is needed and the effects become far from benign, often leading to serious crimes being committed by the users, both directly from the effects of the drug and indirectly

Pierre-Joseph Redouté, 'Opium Poppy', from *Choix des plus belles fleurs . . .* (1827–34).

because of efforts to meet the expense. Drugs have contributed to some of the best (often by accident) and the worst in human history.

Some of the properties of opium have been known about since at least the ancient Egyptians and probably since the earliest civilizations in Mesopotamia. Its influence has been huge, and mostly unedifying. It has had a big influence on poetry and other writing, music and film, provoked at least two wars, provided invaluable

Mary Delany,
*The Opium Poppy*,
1776, collage with
watercolour.

drugs for medical use in at least two other major military conflicts
and a huge market in hallucinatory illegal drugs.

The poppy that produces opium is a quite different species from
the scarlet corn poppy. The opium poppy, *Papaver somniferum* (literal
meaning of the Latin is the 'sleep-making poppy'), is a larger, more
robust plant and its stems and leaves are very glaucous, that is, with
a bluish sheen all over them. The flowers are most commonly violet,
purple, pink or white and nearly always with a dark centre, although
red varieties with a rather darker colour than corn poppies do occur.
Nobody would mistake an opium poppy for a corn poppy when it is
seen growing. Despite this, in paintings opium poppies have often
been depicted as scarlet, largely because of the name association. It
is an annual plant, like the corn poppy, and grows usually to about
1 m (3 ft) in height, occasionally to 1.5 m (5 ft). The opium poppy

is not normally an agricultural weed, though it turns up in gardens and waste sites.

The opium poppy has been so widely planted that, like the corn poppy, it is difficult to work out where it may have come from originally. It is only known in cultivation, or as a casual weed in places that have been cultivated or otherwise disturbed by humans. The likelihood is that, again like the corn poppy, it comes originally from southwestern Asia and the eastern Mediterranean and may have a hybrid origin. Its nearest relative is probably the poppy of Troy, *Papaver setigerum* – a plant that occurs all round the Mediterranean, but contains only trace quantities of opium – or the Iranian poppy, *Papaver bracteatum*. Both of these have been suggested as possible

Opium poppy in Sussex, showing the glaucous leaves and stems and the unripe capsules that can produce the opium.

One of the possible ancestors of the opium poppy,
the Iranian poppy, *Papaver bracteatum*.

parental species of the opium poppy. The opium poppy appears to be diploid but has 22 chromosomes, a unique number among the poppies. It is possible that some hybridization in the early ancestry of the opium poppy has become stabilized at this number.[1] The poppy of Troy is tetraploid with 44 chromosomes. Chromosomes in plants have often been recorded as doubling, but not halving, so from this evidence the poppy of Troy could be a derivative species from the opium poppy and not the other way round. The two species can hybridize occasionally.[2]

Nobody knows quite how widely distributed the opium poppy was as a native plant as it has been spread by people for several thousand years. Especially productive varieties will have been selected over millennia. It seems entirely possible that it has been cultivated for so long that it has become, in effect, a distinct species that has only ever been in cultivation and as a casual weed of cultivated land.

Opium comes from the latex of unripe seed-pods, the fruits of the poppy. It is collected by scoring the fruits with a shallow cut, these days usually with a three- or four-bladed knife, the blades 3 mm or so apart. White latex oozes out and dries into a yellow deposit that is scraped off and can be dried as raw opium. This can, ideally, be done three or four times per pod at intervals of two to three days. That way yield is maximized and 1 hectare (2.5 acres) of opium poppies can produce up to 12 kg (26.5 lb) of opium in a year.[3]

The best-known and most important drug in opium is morphine, used widely in medicine as a strong analgesic. Morphine was the first drug isolated from opium, and actually the first drug ever isolated from a plant, in 1804.[4] It is not the only analgesic or psychoactive drug in opium. There are two other main alkaloid drugs, codeine with analgesic and hallucinatory properties, and thebaine, a stimulatory drug in its unrefined form but which, when chemically altered,

A cut opium poppy seed-pod oozing opium.

Late 19th-century
Bayer & Co.
commercial
heroin bottle.

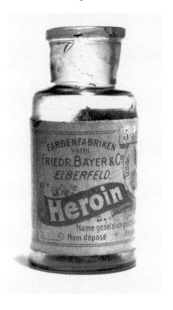

can produce a number of narcotic alkaloids. There are other drugs
in opium such as the vaso-dilating drug papaverine, used mainly in
treating gut spasms, and narcotine, with similar but milder properties to morphine, and some other alkaloids without any of these
properties. The quantities of these drugs in the seed-heads is
remarkably variable. Selective breeding over many centuries has
produced plants with up to 91 per cent of the raw opium consisting
of the three main drugs, although the quantity can be as low as
14 per cent.

Much work has gone into refining these raw substances and
modifying them chemically to produce more potent forms. Drugs
that are present in opium or derive from it are known as opiates.
Morphine can be processed chemically to form heroin, which has
around 2.2 times the potency.[5] Heroin was first commercially produced by the German pharmaceutical company Bayer, in 1895,
though it had been synthesized first in 1874 in St Mary's Hospital in
London. Bayer called it 'heroin' because it was seen to have 'heroic
effects' on its users. Some other opiates with medical uses have been
refined from morphine.

Thebaine is the least known of the three drugs found naturally in opium but, recently, it has been used as the base for synthesizing the analgesics, oxycodone, hydrocodone and hydromorphone and others, as well as codeine. Unlike morphine, thebaine is found in the roots of the opium poppy as well as the seed-pods, and has been extracted from the roots of two other species: both the oriental poppy, *Papaver orientale*, commonly grown as a garden ornamental, and the Iranian poppy, which may be a wild relative of the opium poppy. Some analgesics refined from thebaine have been recorded as up to one thousand times more powerful than morphine. Opioids, chemically similar to the opiates found in the poppy, and with similar effects, have been made chemically since the 1930s. These include the well-known drugs methadone and pethidine. All these opiates and opioids are potentially addictive.

The opium poppy may be by far the best producer of opium because it has been bred for it. Selection of the most potent forms of it will have been made ever since its properties were first discovered. Several other poppy species contain trace quantities of opiates, but none has sufficient concentration for any form of commercial production.

Opium has two main effects in addition to its well-known narcotic/hallucinatory properties. It gives the taker constipation,[6] which led to its prescription for diarrhoea, dysentery and other gut disorders, and it affects the respiratory system, giving it its uses for relieving coughs. It was not a cure for these ailments but could relieve the symptoms. It has been prescribed for many more ailments, including heart problems, sleeplessness or any unknown problem causing pain, but temporary relief was largely through its narcotic properties. It can also have the effect of contracting the iris of the eye. The dangers of overdose have long been known and it has regularly caused accidental deaths or deliberate suicides.

The quantity of opium produced has varied considerably over the centuries. It probably peaked in the early years of the twentieth century when production was around 41,000 tonnes per year. By

A field of opium planted for medicinal use, in Trevino in the Basque country.

2002 this had fallen to 4,000 tonnes, largely because the main source, Afghanistan, had come under the rule of the Taliban who banned growing it.[7] Production in Afghanistan plummeted by more than 90 per cent. It has increased again since then, but there is at the time of writing not enough being produced to meet medical demand.[8] Afghanistan is the biggest producer, but Burma (Myanmar) and parts of Central and South America also produce quantities for export. Formerly, several European countries and the USA were important producers. In 2006 the drug company Macfarlan Smith (a Johnson Matthey company) was allowed to cultivate opium poppies in Britain for medical use. They currently do so under strict conditions on sites in Dorset, Hampshire, Oxfordshire and Lincolnshire.

## A Brief History of Opium Use

Our propensity for trying out the properties of the local plants is certainly great. If something has an effect on the nervous system, be it as a painkiller, stimulant, depressant or hallucinatory, we go to great lengths to find it and use it. Usually it will first be used in rituals, and many of these plants have become associated with religious rituals of one sort or another. So it is with opium, and the evidence suggests that the opium poppy began to be cultivated and used by civilizations from earliest times.[9] Seeds have been found in Neolithic tombs from several parts of Europe dating from around 4200 BC, with many more in the Bronze Age and later.

The early civilizations of the Middle East, from the Sumerians of ancient Mesopotamia in what is now Iraq, to the Assyrians, the Egyptians, Indians, Minoans and others, all used opium. There is evidence of systematic cultivation of it at least since 3500 BC in Sumerian Mesopotamia as it is mentioned on a clay tablet, as part of what was, in effect, a pharmacopoeia. The later Assyrian people of Mesopotamia were familiar with the medicinal properties of many plants. Opium featured, as we would expect, and there is some evidence from the few fragmentary written sources that we have of the use of opium for all sorts of ailments and conditions, from simple headaches to bruises, pregnancy complications and stomach problems.

It is always hard to interpret ancient texts or sculptures, and even in Assyria the evidence is somewhat disputed, but in ancient Egypt the evidence is much stronger. One of the clearest associations comes from the famous tomb of Tutankhamun, dating from around 1300 BC, and excavated in 1922. Tutankhamun was, famously, the boy king of Egypt, coming to reign at the age of nine or ten. He was the sickly son of the previous Egyptian pharaoh (or king) by the pharaoh's own sister. Tutankhamun himself married his half-sister with whom he had two stillborn children, perhaps unsurprisingly given the extent of the incest. He died at the age of seventeen or eighteen and was buried alongside his children with treasures, among them many amulets, some including the characteristic Egyptian 'winged scarab'. Some of these had, unmistakably, poppy capsules underneath. The centrepiece of the amulets is the scarab, or dung beetle, *Scarabaeus sacer*, sacred to the ancient Egyptians, symbolizing creation and resurrection.[10] Dung beetles find dung and cut it into round balls that they roll along the ground, usually in straight lines, before burying them and either laying eggs in them or simply feeding on them. They can roll dung balls that are much heavier than themselves. This behaviour linked the beetle to Ra, or Khepri, the Egyptian sun god, who rolled the sun through the day and over the horizon, only to bring it back in the morning. With this image, the beetle became the earthly symbol of Ra, rolling the dung ball in a way reminiscent of the turning of the earth. Since Ra resurrected the sun again every morning, so the beetle became a symbol of resurrection. An addition to the magical association was the belief by the Egyptians, and later the Greeks, that the beetles were all male and fertilized the dung balls, which acted as mother. The beetle larvae live entirely off the dung, and young beetles emerge fully formed from the dung balls. So why are poppies associated with the sacred scarab in the amulet? It seems almost certain that these are opium poppies and that they represent the sleep, perhaps of death, to be coupled with the idea of resurrection from the scarab.

The tomb of Kha, dating from slightly earlier than Tutankhamun, around 1380 BC (and excavated earlier, in 1906) had many artefacts, and there were some reports of morphine, but this has been refuted,[11] and currently there is no clear evidence of opium use from this tomb.

On Crete archaeologists have found a terracotta figurine that they have dubbed the 'Poppy goddess', now in the museum at Heraklion

Minoan 'poppy goddess' from 1400–1100 BC, a stylized figurine with opium poppy pods in her hair.

and dating from after the main flowering of the Minoan civilization that created the great palaces of Knossos, Phaestos and others. It dates from somewhere between 1400 and 1100 BC, a time when Crete had been subdued by Mycenae and had become a Mycenaean outpost. The figurine is larger than earlier Minoan figures and is much more highly stylized. She is holding up her hands in a gesture of greeting or possibly blessing. There are fruit capsules of the opium poppy on her head. It is not clear whether these depict sleep, death or hallucination, but as they are opium poppies it appears that they are not depicting fertility.

## Classical Greece and Rome

In the works of the Greek writers there are many references to the poppy, and mainly this is to opium. Hippocrates (*c.* 460–377 BC), as we would expect, mentioned the poppy many times in his medical tracts.[12] He distinguishes between the properties of the different-coloured poppies and mentions the potency of 'poppy juice' and its use as a narcotic. Aristotle too refers to its properties as a drug. Many writers warned of the dangers of the poppy – it is, after all, highly poisonous. It is interesting, in this context, that Heraclides of Pontus, writing in 340 BC, refers to the use of opium in euthanasia.[13] Evidently the region was very healthy and people lived to old age, so some, especially women, would use poppy, or hemlock, to kill themselves before they became too infirm or disabled.

The Greeks decorated their gods of sleep (Hypnos), night (Nox) and death (Thanatos) with wreaths of opium poppies, usually as seed-heads, so it is clear that opium poppies are intended. Hypnos is depicted pouring out the opium. One of the first of the world's botanists, Theophrastus, in the third century BC mentions 'meconion' and describes opium's power. Subsequently the famous Greek physician Galen, when working in Rome around AD 180, wrote so eloquently about its powers that it became very popular in Rome.[14]

A plant with such potent powers was always likely to be used in ritual and be given particular significance. In some ancient civilizations its use was restricted to priests or magicians. It was widely used as an analgesic for warriors and in medical practice, especially in surgery. The Egyptians recorded its use to stop babies crying, at which one would guess it would be extremely effective. They also used it with hemlock to lead someone to a painless death.

The passage in Homer's *Odyssey*, where Odysseus and his men find the 'lotus-eaters' on an island off North Africa, appears to refer to a fruit. This has been identified, from Herodotus, as *Ziziphus lotus*, a spiny shrub with edible fruits related to the jujube, but it is not narcotic. The only possible plant with a name that could be regarded

*Nepenthes alata,* a modern-day pitcher-plant in Linnaeus' classification.

as 'lotus', and with narcotic properties, is the blue water lily, *Nymphaea caerulea*. This is not the sacred lotus, an unrelated plant, although it looks and grows like a water lily. The blue water lily was important to the ancient Egyptians and can be processed into a soporific, but the effects are mild. Homer records the effects of inducing sleep and a withdrawal from the cares of the world, and this sounds far more like a reference to opium. Homer appears to have mixed several plants together to provide the symptoms he describes for his lotus-eaters. He refers later to Helen giving Telemachus a drug to forget his grief, calling this 'Nepenthes', which means literally 'not grief' or 'not sorrow' – in other words, an ancient antidepressant. It is now the scientific name for the pitcher-plants of Southeast Asia, deliberately selected by Linnaeus from Homer because 'What

## An early Indian legend[15]

Long ago on the banks of the River Ganges lived a *rishi*. A mouse shared his hut. Since the mouse was afraid of cats, he requested the *rishi* to turn him into a cat. On becoming a cat, dogs started troubling him and so he sought another transformation, but now into a dog. This wish too was granted. However, his troubles continued which he tried to overcome by seeking further transformation such as those into a monkey, boar, elephant and then finally, into a beautiful maiden. This beautiful maiden, called Postomoni, married a king, but soon after fell into a well and died. The aggrieved king turned to the *rishi* for solace. The rishi promised to make his wife immortal, and converted her body into *posto* or the poppy plant. The *rishi* said, 'A capsule of this plant will produce opium. Men will take it greedily. Whosoever partakes of it will acquire a particular trait of each of the animals into which Postomoni was transformed. In other words, the consumer of the capsule will turn out to be as mischievous as a mouse, as fond of milk as a cat, as quarrelsome as a dog, as unclean as a monkey, as savage as a boar, as strong as an elephant and, as spirited as a queen!'

botanist would not be filled with admiration if, after a long journey, he should find this wonderful plant?'[16] Ancient Greek Nepenthes included opium. Tennyson took up Homer's ideas in his poem 'The Lotos-eaters' (1832). He describes a fruit like that of Homer, but, clearly seeing a connection, includes the line: 'And from the craggy ledge the poppy hangs in sleep.'

The Greek myth of Endymion was a popular story for Roman sculptors. Endymion was put to perpetual sleep by Zeus because

Selene fell in love with Endymion while he slept; or, in some versions, Zeus put him to sleep as punishment for trying to sleep with Hera, Zeus's wife. Selene visited him anyway and bore him fifty children. Some Roman sarcophagi depict Endymion with sleep-inducing poppy capsules. Other Roman connections may be with Ceres and the mixing up of the two meanings of poppies.

The properties of opium were not lost on the 'golden age' of the Middle East. Avicenna, the Persian author of the *Canon of Medicine*, writing in the early eleventh century, recommended opium for various ailments including diarrhoea and eye problems.[17] His influence was great and use of the drug spread rapidly. This may have been in part because of the ban on alcohol in the Muslim world, making the lure of opium particularly great. Arab opium traders profited, and widespread use travelled to India and beyond around that time.

## Opium and China

Extensive use, and some of the best-known stories about opium, started in China in the fifteenth century. Opium had been introduced into China some time before that, probably by Arab traders

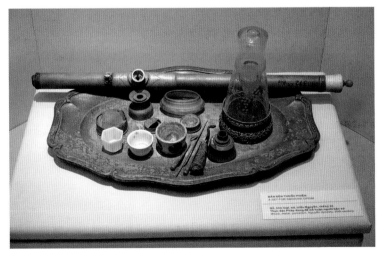

A set of instruments used for smoking opium, on display in a Vietnamese museum.

in the third century AD, perhaps earlier. By the fifteenth century opium was still rare and much sought after, but gradually a trade grew, and by the seventeenth century it was being imported in some quantity. It was often smoked in a mixture with the recently discovered tobacco brought in by explorers from the New World. Its properties became well known and, perhaps inevitably at some stage, it was associated with sex, with the thought that it would 'arrest seminal emission', so that 'lay people use it for the art of sex', an idea going back to 1483 and the writer Xu Boling.[18] The Chinese took keenly to opium; so much so that the emperors regarded it as a real problem and became concerned about its general availability. In 1729 the emperor passed a law prohibiting the sale and the smoking of it except for medical uses. This appears to have had almost no effect at all on the trade, which not only continued, but continued to increase. By the end of the eighteenth century China was selling large quantities of silk, tea and spices to Britain, but trade the other way was very small and it was all paid for in silver. With the supply of silver being limited, Britain needed something else. Opium became that product.[19]

The ever-increasing number of opium addicts in China led, in 1799, to the emperor making the trade and cultivation of opium illegal. By then the trade was becoming lucrative for Britain and it has been estimated that there were more than four million addicts in China. Opium poppies grew well in parts of British India and there were some extensive opium plantations. The East India Company, effectively a British government monopoly, controlled the trade from Britain, and they took to selling opium in large quantities to China. Because the trade was illegal in China a loophole had to be found. That proved not so difficult. There was a cabal of Chinese merchants who were not attached to the government, all trading via the port of Canton, modern-day Guangzhou, in the south. The Chinese authorities had kept Canton open as the one port where 'foreign' traders were allowed to do business. Of course this should not have included opium, but the merchants bribed officials to keep

William John Huggins, *The Opium Ships at Lintin, China 1824*, 1838, oil on canvas.

quiet and the trade continued to flourish. Unsurprisingly under such circumstances, there was a great deal of corruption, with protection rackets and rivalries between the various merchants and their suppliers, all reminiscent of today's mafia, and largely for the same reason: opium was lucrative.

In 1834 the East India Company monopoly was stopped by a Free Trade agreement, and other traders brought the price down. The effect of this was an increase in the quantity sold, and at this point Britain attempted to get China to legalize the trade, to no avail. Throughout the trading, only the port of Canton had been available, and effective opium trade could only flourish under cover. There were not just restrictions imposed on the ports for all foreign traders but other restrictions on how they could trade and with whom. Since opium was the single largest import from Britain, and any trade Britain had with China depended on opium to pay for the highly desirable goods coming the other way, such as tea and silk, diplomacy was already seriously strained. The combination of the trading restrictions and the bribery meant that all foreign traders were seen as second class and not fit for proper diplomacy by both the

Chinese authorities and the merchants themselves. In fact it seems that both sides in this conflict regarded the other as beneath them. This undoubtedly led to a gradual increase in tension, as leaders of both sides greatly resented the sense of inferiority imposed by the other side.

By 1839 as the imports of opium reached new heights, the emperor finally decided to stop the trade altogether. Needless to say, the British would not hand over their wares, so in March 1839 the Chinese officials barricaded the streets and river of Canton. The merchants dealing with the illegal opium had little choice but to hand it over. It amounted to 20,000 boxes of opium, or around 1,200 tonnes. All of this was then destroyed by throwing it into large trenches and siphoning it all into the bay. The destruction of the opium boxes was the final straw. It led to the so-called 'First Opium War' of 1839–42.[20] It is certainly unedifying to think that the war was caused entirely by the trade in a drug that we would now regard as illegal and dangerous. Selling it to the Chinese may have been lucrative, but everyone knew it was dangerous. The British government simply saw the trade, and saw that encouraging addiction in the Chinese fuelled that trade, the inevitable thought being that these people were of secondary importance to the pursuit of profit. No wonder the Chinese saw the trade as a slight on them. Having said that, everything we hear about the illegal drug trade today shows a similar level of corruption and a comparable disregard for the people involved either in the trade or as addicts.

After a few skirmishes, the First Opium War started in earnest when British warships destroyed or damaged much of the Chinese fleet of war junks. The British government put considerable fire-power behind the war, with the British commander, Captain Charles Elliott, demanding compensation for the loss of the opium. Over the next three years Britain took control of considerable areas of southern China, including as far north as the strategically important port of Shanghai on the south side of the Yangtze river delta. The Chinese were defeated, and the prestige of the ruling Qing dynasty was badly dented by the war. Eventually the treaty of Nanking was signed in 1842.

The upshot of the Chinese defeat was a resumption of opium trading, the treatment of British traders and diplomats as equals, and the start of a long decline of the Qing dynasty's powers. Canton had been the only port open to foreign traders but now, as the victors in the war, Britain dictated new terms. The most important gain, finally agreed in 1843, was the ceding of Hong Kong to Britain as a trading port. In addition it was agreed that Shanghai and a few smaller ports were to be opened up to British merchants and their families and not subject to Chinese law. Subsequently other European countries were also given trading rights. The British government demanded full trading rights for all British ships throughout China.

British ships were allowed to trade freely, and by the mid-1850s Chinese ships were being given status as British if registered in Hong Kong so that they could be freed of any restrictions that they would otherwise have had. This clearly irked the Chinese authorities, who felt the humiliation of the earlier defeat strongly, and they started reneging on some of the trade agreements that had been signed after the first war. One such instance was the cargo ship *Arrow*, crewed by Chinese workers but flying the British flag. In October 1856 Chinese marines attacked this ship, which had been accused of piracy, and imprisoned the crew. Although they were released after pressure from the British authorities in the region, the British attacked Canton anyway. When news came back to Britain, justifications of the attack on Canton caused considerable controversy in parliament with the Whigs supporting the Chinese cause. It triggered the dissolution of parliament and a new election, though this was won by the Tories. Hostilities resumed, and what followed became known as the Second Opium War.

Despite the dubious justification for the war, France intervened to help as a result of the murder of a French missionary, Father, now Saint, Auguste Chapdelaine, in 1856, and the USA and Russia both sent envoys with offers of support. China was finally defeated when

Opium smokers in China, 1880. Photograph by Lai Afong.

the British attacked Beijing and destroyed some of the emperor's palaces. The results were far-reaching. First, traders and missionaries were allowed to move and trade freely across the whole of China. Second, Kowloon on the mainland adjacent to Hong Kong was given to Britain in addition to Hong Kong. Finally, opium was legalized. China started growing it itself, and by the turn of the twentieth century was harvesting some 30,000 tonnes of its own opium as well as importing more. It is estimated that one-quarter of the Chinese population regularly took opium. Shanghai remained the main centre of the opium trade and became notorious in the early twentieth century for its low life associated with opium dens, especially gambling and prostitution. This finally came to an end with the communist takeover after the Second World War.

Opium, then, was directly responsible for the British annexation of Hong Kong and its resulting huge wealth as a trading post through which Chinese and other Asian goods reached the rest of the world and China imported goods from elsewhere. Hong Kong remained in British hands for 155 years, until the formal handover to China on 1 July 1997. With the opening up of trade with the rest of the world, the opium wars also stimulated the transportation of large numbers of indentured Chinese labourers to America. As cheap labour, they provided a huge workforce for building the trans-continental railway across the United States in the 1860s that brought such wealth to America.

## Opium in Europe

In Europe opium had come gradually into circulation in intellectual circles. The Swiss physician known as Paracelsus (1493–1541) took opium himself and sang its praises, regarding it as his 'secret remedy'.[21] He was perhaps the first to dissolve opium in alcohol to produce what he called laudanum, after the Latin *laudare*, 'to praise'. Seventeenth-century England's most well-known and respected physician, Thomas Sydenham (1624–1689), strongly advocated its use for coughs and, especially, for dysentery and diarrhoea, saying that: 'Among the remedies which it has pleased Almighty God to give man to relieve his sufferings, none is so universal and efficacious as opium.'[22] He provided the following recipe, largely to cover the bitterness of straight laudanum: 'Opium, 2 ounces; saffron, 1 ounce; bruised cinnamon and bruised cloves, each 1 drachm [3.5 g/⅛ oz]; sherry wine, 1 pint. Mix and macerate for 15 days and filter. Twenty drops are equal to one grain of opium.' By the eighteenth century it was being prescribed for many ailments. Following the ancient Egyptian practice, it was given in dilute form to children, mainly to keep them quiet. This, now obvious to us, was highly dangerous and led to many deaths. At this stage it was considered by governments as a medicine and so was not taxed, unlike alcohol, so was often used by the working classes for a cheap 'high'. No wonder, then, that there were many accidental deaths among adults as well.

One of opium's most vociferous advocates was the Scottish physician John Brown (1735–1788). He had a theory that some diseases were 'over-stimulating' and some 'under-stimulating' and his prescriptions were for a sedative for the over-stimulating ones, and laudanum as a stimulant for the under-stimulating diseases. His foibles are perhaps best described by Thomas Beddoes, the translator of his *Elements of Medicine* (Brown wrote in Latin). In the prefatory description of Brown, Beddoes stated:

> One of his pupils informs me that when he found himself
> languid, he sometimes placed a bottle of whisky in one
> hand and a phial of laudanum on the other; and that
> before he began his lecture he would take forty or fifty
> drops of laudanum in a glass of whisky; repeating the dose
> four or five times during the lecture. Between the effects

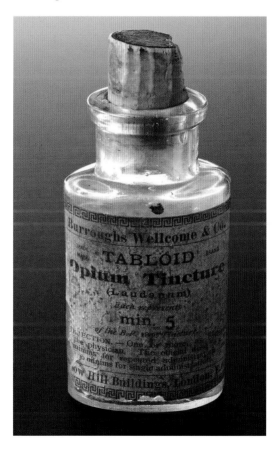

Bottle of
'opium tincture'
or laudanum,
of *c.* 1880–1940.

of these stimulants and voluntary exertion, he soon
waxed warm, and by degrees his imagination was exalted
into phrenzy.[23]

It can be expected that he was affected in such a way – either that or
he would have had problems remaining upright!

In the early nineteenth century we find the most widespread
and well-known use of opium in Europe. It had penetrated into the

Gustave Doré's illustration of opium smoking for
Charles Dickens's unfinished novel *Edwin Drood* (1870).

fashionable salons by then and several writers were famous opium-takers, such as Charles Dickens, Wilkie Collins, Arthur Conan Doyle, Jules Verne, Alexandre Dumas and Thomas de Quincey, along with the poets Samuel Taylor Coleridge, George Crabbe, Elizabeth Barrett Browning, Charles Baudelaire and, at least occasionally, John Keats. Hector Berlioz said that he composed his *Symphonie fantastique* in 1830 under the influence of opium. Even Queen Victoria herself took it to ease menstrual cramps.

The most explicit of these was the journalist and essayist Thomas de Quincey. He gained notoriety, retained to this day, for his 'Confessions of an English Opium-eater' of 1821, first published in the *London Magazine*, later republished in book form, usually with some of his other essays.[24] The title has deliberate echoes of St Augustine's famous *Confessions* and is autobiographical in a similar way. This long essay lays out the wonders and the horrors of taking and becoming addicted to opium, but also includes personal anecdotes and comments on society. He suggests that he is the one person he knows who has been able to give opium up – to 'have untwisted, almost to its final links, the accursed chain that fettered me' – but, as with nearly all addicts, he returned to it, especially after his wife died. He was friends with the Romantic poet Coleridge, another famous addict, and stayed with him and William Wordsworth in the Lake District. He was perennially short of money, partly through having eight children and, of course, because of his opium addiction. He has been blamed for extolling the virtues of opium and encouraging people to try it.

A later opium-user was Francis Thompson (1859–1907), who published his poem 'The Poppy' in 1891 when he was an addict. This has twenty stanzas and starts with the following description of the flower:

> Summer set lip to earth's bosom bare,
> And left the flush'd print in a poppy there;
> Like a yawn of fire from the grass it came,
> And the fanning wind puff'd it to flapping flame.

With burnt mouth red like a lion's it drank
The blood of the sun as he slaughter'd sank,
And dipp'd its cup in the purpurate shine
When the eastern conduits ran with wine.

Till it grew lethargied with fierce bliss,
And hot as a swinked gipsy is,
And drowsed in sleepy savageries,
With mouth wide a-pout for a sultry kiss.

As so often happens, the two poppy species are mixed up. The poem continues with a likening of the poppy's short-lived and crumpled flower to love and its loss, as well as wasted years of opium addiction.

Perhaps the most famous literary creation that came from an opium trance is one of Samuel Taylor Coleridge's best-known poems, 'Kubla Khan'. Incomplete, and described by Coleridge as a 'fragment', the fantastical imagery of the poem does indeed suggest an opium dream. It was famously interrupted by the 'Person from Porlock', who woke Coleridge from his trance and stopped him from completing the poem. John Keats's 'Ode to a Nightingale' is thought to have been influenced by the effects of opium with, again, some vivid imagery ('blushful Hippocrene / with beaded bubbles winking at the brim, and purple-stained mouth'), and its references to a 'dull opiate', a 'draught of vintage' and the desire to 'fade far away, dissolve, and quite forget . . . the weariness, the fever'.[25] Keats mentions the narcotic effect of poppies directly elsewhere, most clearly in another of his best-known poems, the 'Ode to Autumn': 'Or in the half-reaped furrow sound asleep, / Drowsed with the fume of poppies'. Opium continued to be praised both for its medicinal and its hallucinatory effects throughout the nineteenth century.

It is instructive, in the context of nineteenth-century Britain, to recall the famous reference to religion as 'the opium of the people' by Karl Marx. Nearly everyone today sees this as a reference to Marx's idea that religion is simply a drug that subjugates people to passivity with false hopes and dreams similar to those induced by taking opium. But Marx wrote that line in 1843, just a year after the end of the First Opium War, and the context gives it a quite different flavour: 'Religion is the sigh of the oppressed creature, the heart of a heartless world, and the spirit of a spiritless situation. It is the opium of the people.' Marx himself took opium, and it was not only legal at the time but regarded as an important medicine. To his audience his remark would have strong overtones of both medical effectiveness and of conflict, as well as of a bringer of passivity and dreams.[26]

## Opium in North America

North America was as much under opium's spell as Europe was, especially during the nineteenth century. Edgar Allan Poe was a famous user and advocate, as was Benjamin Franklin, who took it as a remedy for kidney stones, though one suspects the main effect was analgesic. Oliver Wendell Holmes (1809–1894), the American

Birthday cake inspired by *The Wizard of Oz*, depicting Judy Garland as Dorothy with her companions in the sea of poppies.

physician, poet and academic, sang the praises of opium in 1860 in an address to the Massachusetts Medical Society. He advocated throwing out most drugs and medications, suggesting that if all 'could be sunk to the bottom of the sea, it would be all the better for mankind – and all the worse for the fishes'. Nevertheless, 'We can make an exception for opium, which the Creator himself seems to prescribe . . . A little opium, it helps the imagination.'[27]

A slightly later writer to include poppies was L. Frank Baum in *The Wizard of Oz*, first published in 1900. He may have got his inspiration for Dorothy and her companions falling asleep in a poppy field from Keats's image in the 'Ode to Autumn'. He depicts the field (as usual, with the two poppy species mixed up) as very dangerous for Dorothy and her dog, Toto, sending them to a sleep from which they could not wake up. Dorothy needed her companions, the Scarecrow and the Tin Man, who had not flesh bodies and therefore were not affected by the opium, to pull her and Toto from their sleeping state. The film of Baum's story, made in 1939 with Judy Garland, has become much better known than the book and, as so often with films, softens the image considerably. In the film the good witch breaks the spell of the poppies, so Dorothy and Toto can wake up. The image remains popular and has been used for many purposes.

If opium was popular by the mid-nineteenth century, it was to take on a whole new significance in the years that followed, because between 1861 and 1865 America suffered its defining conflict in the devastating Civil War.[28] In previous conflicts, opium and its derivatives had been used as essential analgesics and narcotics for pain relief, but it took on a far greater importance during this war. This was partly because of the sheer scale of the conflict, and partly because the wounds that the soldiers suffered were so great. Weaponry had become much more sophisticated, with grenades and shrapnel causing terrible suffering. Limbs were amputated almost routinely, and opium was almost always the medicine of choice. It could, as we have seen, also help in at least alleviating the symptoms of diarrhoea and dysentery, which then, as later, were among the biggest killers of the war. Opium was given out at every opportunity, to be used as an ointment as well as to be ingested. It was also used by numerous bereaved widows to provide some relief, albeit temporary, from their hardships.

The importance of opium for the war meant that both sides in the conflict decided to plant their own opium poppies to fill the demand. The result was that large areas were planted in several states on both the Union and Confederate sides. The addictive effects of opium were well known by this time but there is little documentation of addiction in American society following the Civil War. This has come as a surprise to many people, and there must have been addicts after the war treating themselves with opium or its derivatives to alleviate the continued suffering from war wounds. It is possible, though, that after the conflict many people did not need the narcotic effects and simply settled back to a civilian existence. Although opium is addictive, each person must have a reason for taking it. After the end of the war that reason may have largely disappeared for the soldiers. This is a well-documented occurrence from after the Vietnam conflict a century later.

The American public was shocked by the findings, in 1971, that most of the soldiers who had fought in Vietnam during the previous decade of war had tried drugs during it, first marijuana and later heroin, though both were illegal. At least 40 per cent of servicemen had tried heroin and 15 to 20 per cent appeared to be addicted to it while stationed in Vietnam. Some of these people were followed up after their return, as the American government and its people suspected that they were in for a serious drug problem. What happened surprised everyone. More than 95 per cent of the takers had stopped using heroin within a year of returning to America.[29] A few had transferred to other drugs, mainly amphetamines or barbiturates, but most had stopped altogether. The best predictor of continued drug use by servicemen was whether they had used drugs before going to Vietnam. The overall number of people taking drugs may have gone up a little, and drugs were more widely available (if illegal), but the proportion of servicemen using drugs quickly decreased to that of society as a whole. The conclusion was that the settled and quite different environment back home meant that drugs were no longer necessary for the majority of servicemen. It suggests too that for regular drug users in society today, a change in environment may be the most useful treatment.

## The Twentieth Century

Opium always had its detractors, especially when associated with the opium wars with China, and by the end of the nineteenth century many influential people were beginning to stress the negative side of opium. This had always been known about, but it was not until now that it came to the fore. 'Opium dens' had sprung up and all could see that these were fundamentally places of corruption, shady dealing and prostitution. Oscar Wilde could write of 'opium dens' in *The Picture of Dorian Gray* (1890) as 'dens of horror'.

Eventually the International Opium Convention was drawn up in 1912. This committed the twelve signatory countries, including the USA, China and the UK, to a worldwide ban on trading opium, morphine and cocaine. Britain was, at the time, a rather reluctant signatory, with many thinking that alcohol was the worse problem. Once the First World War had begun, attitudes changed. Drugs were seen as a much greater problem than before and there was emergency legislation and tightening of licences. This resulted, for the first time, in drugs going largely underground. The 1912 Convention was brought fully into force internationally in 1919, and the UK's Dangerous Drugs Act was passed in 1920, banning opium and other drugs altogether. The USA eventually banned the drug even for medical use in 1924, though it is used again now.

Since then morphine, and some other opiates, have remained as vital pain relievers for medical use, but all opiates are illegal for 'recreational use'. Prescriptions for opiates and opioids as painkillers have actually increased in the USA since 2000, despite the fact that prescribing doctors must know that all these are addictive. Although heroin is not actually prescribed itself, many prescription drugs are chemically similar. The number of heroin addicts has been increasing steadily since about 2004, and it is thought that the widespread prescription of opiates to teenagers with sports or other injuries and to many others with minor ailments is a major cause. Heroin is the available street opiate and black-market sellers have cashed in on this market, which now includes people from many walks of life in American society, especially since the economic depression of 2008. It was in that year that drug deaths outnumbered road deaths for the first time, and the number has continued to increase. Recent years appear to have seen a resurgence in the taking of drugs, both heroin and chemically derived drugs such as barbiturates.

# Afghanistan

No description of opium would be complete without considering modern Afghanistan.[30] This extraordinary country, one of the poorest in the world and often described as ungovernable, has been the world's largest supplier of opium for the last several decades. Poppy growing was initially spread right across the country, but of late has centred on the large southern province of Helmand. This is naturally a semi-desert region, and agriculture is mainly based on irrigation from the river Helmand. The irrigation was set up in the 1960s with a dam built with aid from the USA. Russia invaded on 24 December 1979 and ruled the country for a while, but always there were insurgents and strong resistance to the Russians from this fervently Muslim country. Russia finally departed in February 1989, by which time much of the irrigated land of Helmand was given over to poppy production. Other crops are grown in Helmand, such as wheat, tomatoes, cotton, sunflowers, tobacco and several other fruits and staples, all of which can grow well under irrigation. But the problem was, and remains, a simple one: poppies are, now at least, more lucrative than any of these. Indeed they can be much more lucrative, often fetching far more than twice the price for the farmers per unit area.

After the Russians left, the different Muslim factions within the country fought each other. The mujahideen who had, in effect, forced the Russian withdrawal were being taken over by the hard-line Taliban. The Taliban decided that poppy growing was 'un-Islamic' and drastically reduced production during the 1990s, although, prudently for them as it turned out, they kept their existing stocks. But then, in 2001, came the 9/11 attacks in New York by Al-Qaeda. The USA and its coalition partners went into Afghanistan, and Helmand became their central base of operations. One of the first things they did was to try to destroy all the remaining poppy fields. The effect was exactly the opposite of what was intended. Firstly, the price of opium went shooting up and the Taliban, with quite a volte-face over the morality of opium, could sell off their stocks of opium at considerable profit to finance their military operations. And, with the poppy both lucrative and suddenly seeming not quite so un-Islamic after all, many farmers started growing it again. This is a poor country and, though many farmers did not support the Taliban, feeding their families was inevitably the priority and that was achieved more effectively by growing poppies than anything else. They also came under the protection of the Taliban, who found they could extort more money as a protection racket. Poppies were the source of their wealth and they needed the farmers.

Since 2007 there have been several initiatives in Helmand aimed at reducing the poppy crop by encouraging farmers to grow food crops. Some of the irrigation canals that had been destroyed or fallen into disrepair have been rebuilt and fertilizer imported, largely with aid from Britain. Financial incentives have been put in place for the farmers to grow wheat and other food crops again. If they can get enough money from these, the great majority of Afghan farmers would much rather grow them than grow poppies. They know very well that the trade is largely illegal and underground and, ultimately, does no people any favours with the debilitating effects

Poppy field in Helmand province, Afghanistan, with American marines on patrol.

of the narcotic. There is a peculiar irony in the fact that it is mainly heroin addicts in Britain and America who make the poppy fields of Afghanistan so profitable, and that it is troops from those same countries who have suffered so much as a consequence of the addicts' money flowing into Afghanistan.

## Modern Opium

Genetic modification has now come to opium, or at least some of its constituents.[31] The idea is that, if scientists can engineer the genes from the opium poppy that lead to opiate production into a microbe, then manufacture of these for medical use will be much enhanced. So far there has been limited success using the brewer's yeast, *Saccharomyces cerevisiae*. A concoction of microbial and plant enzymes was needed, using the bacterium *Pseudomonas putida* as a go-between, as well as the poppy and yeast. Although the modified yeast has produced thebaine and some of the precursors of morphine, there have been many problems in getting sufficient activity. It is not yet a commercially viable proposition, but may become so.

The opium poppy has provided us with invaluable medical analgesics and, despite the fact that some opioids are now made chemically, is likely to continue to do so for a while yet. Meanwhile the market in illegal heroin is unlikely to disappear any time soon.

## *eight*
# Other Uses and Associations

❧

## The Poppy as Food

'Poppy seeds' are sold for cooking, and the oil that can be extracted from the seeds has many uses. These are normally, although not exclusively, seeds of the opium poppy. Some other poppies can produce similar seeds but the opium poppy is by far the most important, both because it is already cultivated so is more readily available than other species, and because it produces good quantities of edible and tasty seeds that are larger than those of many other poppies, though still tiny compared with many seeds. The seeds are normally blue and have only the slightest traces of any narcotic drug. The most popular varieties today have white seeds, and some yellow as well as blue.

Poppy seed cakes, biscuits and similar have become popular in Britain, after some cookery programmes on television have advocated them. The poppy seeds are usually mixed with fruits, especially lemons or oranges, or almonds, yoghurt or other ingredients. Sometimes they are baked first. They are also used as a topping on bread and rolls and can be used in soups, pastries, salads or in dips or spreads. Poppy seeds give all of these a distinctive, slightly nutty taste. They have long been popular in Germany, Austria, Hungary and other European countries as an ingredient or toppings for strudel or sweet pastry or other desserts. The Czech Republic is, along with Turkey, the world's biggest producer, yielding around 20,000 tonnes per year; 49,000 tonnes in the peak year of 2008 but down

German poppy seed cake, or Stollen.

to 13,900 in 2013. Europe has been responsible for 66 per cent of the total production of poppy seeds between 1993 and 2013.[1]

Poppy seeds are marketed as having health benefits and they are rich in various minerals such as calcium, potassium and iron and in beneficial fatty acids and some vitamins. They are said to help digestive complaints, ulcers, skin problems and heart conditions among other things. In their raw form they can go rancid so they need to be kept cool and dry.

Poppy seeds are known as *khus-khus* in Turkey (not to be confused with the granular wheat-based semolina known as couscous, originating in North Africa and widely used in many countries). Turkey produces a similar amount to that of the Czech Republic, around 20,000 tonnes per year with a peak of 52,000 in 2003; 19,000 in 2013.[2] *Khus-khus* has become an important crop for the country. The quantity and the trade in poppy seeds in Turkey is distorted by illegal imports.[3] These come mainly from Afghanistan and Pakistan, where the growers make their money from producing opium. This means that the seeds are a by-product of the opium trade and can be sold at a much cheaper price than the legal growers demand. Turkey exports up to half the crop to India where the seeds are used in curries. In Turkey itself they are used mainly to make sweet puddings such as halwa and cakes.

There are several poppy species native to Turkey, and the Turkish people have a special relationship with red poppies too. They can be made into rather strikingly coloured beverages and sorbets.[4] These are made from the petals of the corn poppy so are bright red. 'Red poppy syrup' is a traditional syrup made from the petals, and a sorbet can be prepared in a similar way from poppy petals. When preparing either of these, the black petal bases are always removed. Those bases contain a little thebaine, so that is not included in the syrup or sorbet. In fact they do have a very slight narcotic effect with the trace quantities of narcotics that are found in the corn poppy, so can be used as a sleeping aid. They may have a further effect since the petals contain some flavonoids, especially cyanidin B. This substance is also found in red wine and is thought to have a preventative effect on cancer and heart disease.

The poppy in Turkey is also inextricably associated with weddings. We are so used to associating a white dress with a bride that it comes as a surprise that in Turkey, brides traditionally wore red dresses. More recently they have adopted the more widespread white dresses, but these include long red ribbons with the idea that guests fix money to them.[5] This colour is what makes the association with poppies. The Turkish name for a bride is *gelin*; the poppy is *gelincik* – literally, a 'little bride'. Some of this tradition may be waning, but the name remains.

## Poppy Oil

The oil that can be extracted from the seeds is mainly now used as a tasty cooking or salad oil. It is a stable oil and, unlike the raw seeds, does not go rancid quickly and has almost no smell, but has a taste similar to the raw seeds. In the early years of the twentieth century the main producers of the oil were France and Germany, and they imported

German poster of 1916 advocating the planting
of sunflowers and poppies for their oil.

large quantities of poppy seeds from various other countries of Europe and the Middle East. Between them, France and Germany produced up to 60 million kg of oil per year. 'Huile de Pavot', or sometimes simply 'Huile blanche' (white oil), is still sold in France, though it is much rarer than it was in the early twentieth century. As of 2015, one current manufacturer, Bio Planète, claims that it is now using oil from the blue-flowered poppy, *Meconopsis betonicifolia*, in place of an unspecified amount of the opium poppy oil, to give it a 'more intense aroma'. In their advertising, yet again, they mix up the species; the picture on their bottle shows neither of these species – it is a corn poppy![6]

Poppy oil is versatile and, although we have now replaced some of its former uses with other oils, it is still used in medicine as a carrier. One of its main recent uses has been as a carrier for iodine, either where iodine is deficient and people may be prone to growing goitres, or where iodine is used as a radiocontrast agent. A radiocontrast agent is needed to highlight blood or tissue in radiography or X-rays. Iodine in poppy oil has a harmless interaction with the body but can be seen clearly under X-rays. It has been used as a carrier of drugs, particularly those used for tumours in the liver. It seems that it may become concentrated in liver tumours so can be an effective carrier for chemotherapy drugs.[7]

Poppy oil has had several other uses, including as a base for paints, varnishes and soaps, and could even be used in oil lamps. Some painters, in particular, still use poppy oil as their base and it is thought that it has been used in paints as long as oil-based paints have been used, perhaps 1,500 years. When it dries it does not turn as yellow as most other oils and, although it may not last quite as well as others, some regard it as an ideal base for painters' oil or varnish.[8]

## Tall Poppies

The great cause for which Margaret Thatcher was both loved and hated as British prime minister in the 1980s centred around her defence of individual achievement. She wanted to encourage and reward anyone who was prepared to be innovative and stick out of the crowd. Before she became prime minister, she said in a speech to the American Institute of SocioEconomic Studies in New York in September 1975:

> I believe you have a saying in the Middle West: 'Don't cut down the tall poppies. Let them grow tall.' I would say let our children grow tall, and some taller than others if they have the ability to do so. Because we must build a society in which each citizen can develop his full potential, both for his own benefit and for the community as a whole, a society in which originality, skill, energy and thrift are rewarded, in which we encourage rather than restrict the variety and richness of human nature.[9]

The reference to poppies in this context comes originally from the Roman historian Livy (c. BC 60– AD 17), when describing a response from the tyrannical king Tarquinius Superbus (Tarquin the Proud). A messenger had arrived from Tarquin's son Sextus, asking his father what he should do now that he was apparently all-powerful in Gabii. In answer Tarquin said nothing but took a stick and, sweeping it across his garden, cut off the tallest of the poppies growing there. Sextus got the message: kill anyone who may ever be a rival for power or influence in your territory. He killed all the most prominent people and established himself as absolute ruler. The Dutch artist (later settling in England) Lawrence Alma-Tadema painted Tarquinius Superbus with a bed of poppies in front of him in 1867.

Livy's near-contemporary, Virgil, may have picked up the idea, as he mentions in the *Aeneid*, Book 9:

> His snowy neck reclines upon his breast
> Like a fair flower by the keen share oppress'd:
> Like a white poppy sinking on the plain,
> Whose heavy head is overcharged with rain.
> (trans. John Dryden, 1697)

Lawrence Alma-Tadema, *Tarquinius Superbus*,
1867, oil on panel.

Livy was almost quoting a similar story from the Greek historian
Herodotus (*c.* 484–425 BC), discussing the Corinthian ruler Periander
asking advice from Thrasybulus, though here Thrasybulus cuts off
the tallest and best ears of wheat rather than poppies.

The metaphor appears to have been picked up in the eighteenth
century and crossed first to America and then to Australia in the nineteenth century. America, as the land of opportunity, has traditionally
rewarded enterprise, and Margaret Thatcher was surely right when she
picked up the idea in America that you do not cut down the tall poppies but let them grow. (Her own policies explicitly took up the ideas
of the American Nobel Prize-winning economist Milton Friedman.)

In Australia the idea has had a very different reception, and has been much more widely quoted. Historically the Australians have been suspicious of success and, in 1931, the premier of New South Wales, Jack Lang, introduced egalitarian policies by saying he was 'cutting the heads off tall poppies'.[10] Much later, in 2013, the journalist Peter Hartcher of the *Sydney Morning Herald* explained that the national ethos did not permit any Australian to stand out: 'Australia is supposed to be the land of the tall poppy syndrome, where the successful are cut down to the same size as everyone else, quick smart. You're not supposed to stand out for intelligence, achievement or, worst of all, wealth.'[11] This dislike of showiness seems to have passed into the national culture, and the tall-poppy syndrome lives on, although Hartcher's article suggested that some, at least, are tolerated and that Australia may, in this sense, be 'growing up'.

It has been said that the sociologist Max Weber (1864–1920) justified the idea of the tall-poppy syndrome by expressing the opinion that, in many societies, domination is what we might now refer to as a 'zero-sum game', meaning that if one person gained status in that society, it meant that another lost it. Although Weber did suggest that once dominance is established, others have to fall in line and be obedient, he did not suggest that 'cutting down the tall poppies' was necessary to maintain dominance. Indeed, others gaining status could actually lead to a 'positive-sum game' or even a negative-sum one in different situations with many gaining or losing.[12]

In Margaret Thatcher's Britain there is no doubt that the 'tall poppies' did thrive, especially in the financial services industries, which largely replaced the manufacturing industries that had been the source of Britain's wealth before. Their employees' salaries increased by an average of over 60 per cent in real terms during Thatcher's premiership, although the poorest people's salaries actually decreased in real terms at the same time.

# Poppy Land

When the railways were built across Britain in the nineteenth century, many previously isolated places became accessible to city dwellers, especially wealthy Londoners. This meant that writers and critics could widen the scope of their articles for the papers and see many parts of the country that had previously taken too long to reach. So it was that, on a warm August day in 1883, the art and drama critic of the *Daily Telegraph*, Clement Scott (1841–1904), travelled by train to Cromer on the north Norfolk coast. The railway from Norwich to the escarpment on the outskirts of Cromer had been completed in 1877. Cromer was a fishing port at that time but was increasingly being used as a holiday resort, mainly by the locals. A further railway line coming in from the west that stopped in the middle of the town was completed in 1887. By 1883 Scott described 'music and laughter and seaside merriment . . . bands and bathing machines' in the town. He decided to leave the bustle of the town to take a walk along the cliff. He was entranced by what he saw, and the contrast with the town and railway:

> It is difficult to convey an idea of the silence of the fields through which I passed, or the beauty of the prospect that surrounded me – a blue sky without a cloud across it; a sea sparkling under a haze of heat; wild flowers in profusion around me; poppies predominating everywhere.

He came across a ruined church tower at Sidestrand, preserved as a coastal marker on this rapidly eroding coast. The rest of the church had already collapsed and fallen onto the beach or into the sea, and a new church further inland had just been built using flints from the original church. He also found a windmill with a cottage nearby. In the cottage he spied a country girl, Louie Jermy, wearing a bonnet trimmed with poppies, and he enquired of her whether he could stay as he needed lodgings for the night. It turned out that she was a miller's daughter, and they were pleased to put him up. He proceeded to write descriptions for the paper about the countryside and its way of life. He painted it all in idyllic terms, contrasting the slow pace and gentle existence to the urban life of London society.[13] It does not seem to have occurred to him how hard life could be for such people. His articles were read by millions, and fashionable Londoners came to visit in numbers. Many wanted to stay in the miller's house with 'The Maid of the Mill'.

Clement Scott himself visited every year after this until his death. The poppies clearly impressed him as the most noticeable of all the flowers there, and they are abundant in East Anglia still. The idea of immortalizing the region as 'Poppy Land' came from what must be his best-known contribution about it, a poem that most of us would regard as sentimental to the point of sickliness, published in 1885 in *The Theatre* that Scott himself edited. 'The Garden of Sleep' is set in the graveyard beside the ruined tower that he loved:

> On the grass of the cliff, at the edge of the steep,
> God planted a garden – a garden of sleep!
> 'Neath the blue of the sky, in the green of the corn,
> It is there that the regal red poppies are born!
> Brief days of desire, and long dreams of delight,
> They are mine when my Poppy-land cometh in sight.
> In music of distance, with eyes that are wet,
> It is there I remember, and there I forget!
> O! heart of my heart! Where the poppies are born,
> I am waiting for thee, in the hush of the corn.
> Sleep! Sleep!
>    From the cliff to the Deep
>      Sleep, my Poppy Land, Sleep!

> In my garden of sleep, where red poppies are spread,
> I wait for the living alone with the dead!
> For a tower in ruins stands guard o'er the deep,

At whose feet are green graves of dear women asleep!
Did they love as I love, when they lived by the sea?
Did they wait as I wait, for the days that may be?
Was it hope or fulfilling that entered each breast
Ere death gave release and the poppies gave rest?
O! Life of my life! On the cliffs by the sea,
By the graves in the grass I am waiting for thee!
Sleep! Sleep!
    In the dews of the Deep!
      Sleep, my Poppy Land, Sleep!

Was opium as well as the graveyard in Scott's mind? We cannot tell, and Scott's description may only indicate his idyllic vision of the slow pace of life. He certainly publicized this coast and its attractions, eventually publishing a book about it in 1886 called *Poppy-land: Papers Descriptive of Scenery on the East Coast.*[14]

Promoters of tourism in the region saw the potential for this coast and its railway. The idea that it was Poppy Land took hold: the Mill House was re-christened 'Poppyland Cottage'; 'Poppyland china' was produced by a local pottery; 'Poppyland perfume' was introduced and local companies published numerous posters saying 'Welcome to Poppy Land'. The railway to Cromer became known as the Poppy Land railway, later to become the 'Poppy Line'.

Sadly, the heyday of Poppy Land as a tourist destination was not to last. With the advent of the First World War, military officers were billeted in the Mill House and the whole coastline became militarized. Louie's father died in 1916 and Louie herself was evicted by the landlord to become a recluse. Even Clement Scott's church tower did not survive. In February 1916 there was a violent storm and it finally joined the rest of the church in the sea. A replica of this tower was built on the new church.

After the First World War, Cromer ceased to be a resort for fashionable London society and became much frequented by those wanting numerous seaside attractions and nightlife. Today it is perhaps a little faded, but still a thriving seaside resort with much of its Victorian architecture still dominating the town. The railway line between Norwich and Cromer has, perhaps remarkably, survived; it has remained open and reaches beyond Cromer, to Sheringham just to the west. Before reaching the coast, and 'Poppy Land', it skirts the Broads region and this area is well known for its birds, especially in the marshes. The Royal Society for the Protection of Birds has several marshland nature reserves in East Anglia, and has particularly championed one of the region's most charismatic birds, the elusive bittern. The result is that the railway line has become known as the Bittern Line.

Beyond Sheringham the railway line had stopped, a victim of the cuts imposed by Dr Beeching in the 1960s, but reopened as a heritage railway line from Sheringham along the coast westwards towards Weybourne and then inland to Holt, a round trip of about 10 miles. Enthusiasts now run the heritage line with both steam and diesel trains for tourists. They have resuscitated the Poppy Line name for this stretch, even though the original Poppy Land and Poppy Line was further east. The operators make sure there are many poppies lining the track.

In 1984 the director John Madden and writer William Humble teamed up to make a television film based on Clement Scott's trip to Cromer in 1883. They called it, naturally, *Poppyland*, and it was broadcast as part of BBC2's *Screen Two* series on 13 January 1985 with Alan Howard playing Scott.

When the Plantlife charity raised the idea of county flowers in 2002, Norfolk initially chose Alexanders, an edible yellow umbellifer that was probably introduced by the Romans as a potherb. It is common and characteristic of roadsides within a few miles of the coasts of Norfolk and is a suitable alternative. But many locals, perhaps especially those living by Poppy Land, clubbed together and demanded a re-vote, putting forward the poppy as a much more suitable plant. The poppy won the day and the new vote established the poppy as Norfolk's county flower. It was already Essex's county flower.

## Children's Games

Children are adept at making up games with whatever is available. Poppies, being so obvious to any country child, have featured in various games and pastimes. One example was sent to Richard Mabey's *Flora Britannica*. This described how, when poppies were abundant, there had been a tradition of making dolls from poppy flowers:

> The flower petals were folded down to reveal the black
> hairy 'head'. The 'skirt' was kept in place by tying round
> it a piece of fine grass to form a belt. Mature poppies gave
> red dollies, but for pink ones and for white ones,
> the immature buds were opened.

This tradition was revived in the 1980s. It seems a curious tradition, as the flowers last for such a short time and the dolls must have lasted for a matter of hours at best.

One story from the eastern USA has another slant on using poppy petals. A group of girls would arrange a 'poppy show' by gathering poppy petals and arranging them in an elaborate pattern between pieces of glass. When enough were gathered they would be placed on a board and the girls would chant: 'Pinny, pinny, poppy show, Give me a pin and I'll let you know.'[15] This could be done with other flowers but it was always called a poppy show whatever flowers were used. This must have been with introduced corn poppies, which became very common in many parts of the USA. There are, no doubt, other stories and childhood games.

## The Poppy in Love and Death

As discussed earlier, poppies are integral to Turkish weddings, but can be part of wedding bouquets in almost any country – though many poppy species, including the corn poppy, drop their petals so quickly that they are never going to be the most popular choice. Artificial

poppies or poppy-printed dresses are more effective. One British wedding shop in Darlington, County Durham, is called 'Poppy Bridal' with a poppy logo.

The poppy features in Persian literature, sometimes confused with tulips as a symbol of love.[16] It is the eternal lover flower, perhaps partly because it is so ephemeral. It appears to double as a symbol of martyrdom.

Poppies are always noticed wherever they grow, and the poppies of the Americas also have their associations. One association is with the Aztecs in Mexico. Here the native yellow-flowered prickly poppy, *Argemone mexicana*, was a sacred flower to the Aztecs and was included in burials to nourish the dead.[17]

## The Lasting Power of the Poppy as Weed, Symbol, Narcotic and Food

One of the most striking features of poppies, and of the writing on poppies, is the variety of ways in which we have interacted with them. Poppies have featured in so many aspects of our lives both directly and indirectly. The corn poppy, a symbol of cornfields and Remembrance, remains totally bound up with the opium poppy, bringer of sleep.

Some aspects of this relationship can be summed up by a garden cultivar of the opium poppy. This striking-looking poppy was bred initially in the 1880s. There are four dark pink petals that are frilled around the edges, and the centre of the base of each petal is white, so they form a white cross in the middle of the flower. It was named the 'Victoria Cross' variety. It breeds true from seed and is sold by a number of seed merchants. It exemplifies the showiness of the family generally, and at the same time manages to conflate the fact that it is an opium poppy with the overt military connection through its name.

I will leave the last word ('A Poppy') to the Ulster poet Michael Longley:

> When millions march into the mincing machine
> An image in Homer picks out the individual
> Tommy and the doughboy in his doughboy helmet:
> 'Lolling to one side like a poppy in a garden
> Weighed down by its seed capsule and rainwater,
> His head drooped under the heavy, crestfallen
> Helmet' (an image Virgil steals – *lasso papavera*
> *Collo* – and so do I), and so Gorgythion dies,
> And the poppy that sheds its flower-heads in a day
> Grows in one summer four hundred more, which means
> Two thousand petals overlapping as though to make
> A cape for the corn goddess or a soldier's soul.[18]

# Timeline

◊

| | |
|---|---|
| 10,000–8000 BC | Agriculture begins in Mesopotamia (Iraq). Corn poppies probably first evolved as agricultural weed |
| 4000 BC | References to poppies from ancient Mesopotamia |
| 3500–2500 BC | Evidence of corn poppies from Neolithic sites in Britain |
| 2000 BC | Assyrians of Mesopotamia record using opium |
| 1300 BC | Opium poppy capsules depicted on Egyptian amulets |
| 1200 BC | 'Poppy goddess' – a figurine holding opium poppy pods – made in Minoan Crete |
| 400 BC | Hippocrates makes detailed description of opium and distinguishes the different poppy species |
| 400 BC–AD 100 | Greek goddess Demeter and her Roman equivalent Ceres depicted with poppies as symbols of agricultural fertility and of sleep |
| AD 10 | Livy describes Tarquinius Superbus cutting the heads off 'tall poppies' |
| 1025 | Avicenna in *Canon of Medicine* recommends opium for many ailments |
| 16th–18th century | Huge increase in opium use in China |

| | |
|---|---|
| 1676 | Thomas Sydenham publishes *Medical Observations* in England, introducing a recipe for laudanum as an almost universal analgesic and medicine |
| 1804 | Morphine refined from opium |
| 19th century | Opium taken by numerous well-known writers, composers and others in Europe and America, including Queen Victoria |
| 19th century | Many ornamental poppies introduced to Europe including California poppy, tree poppies and, by 1860, blue poppies from the Himalayas |
| 1815 | Poppies said to have come up in profusion after the Battle of Waterloo |
| 1821 | Thomas de Quincey first publishes 'Confessions of an English Opium-eater' |
| 1839–42 | First Opium War, fought between the United Kingdom and China's Qing Empire leading to Hong Kong ceding to Britain |
| 1857–9 | Second Opium War between the British Empire and China, leading to Kowloon being added to British Hong Kong territory. All was returned in 1997 |
| 1861–4 | Opium widely used in the American Civil War and grown by both sides |
| 1873 | Monet paints *Coquelicots at Argenteuil* and subsequently more landscapes with poppies |
| 1879 | Revd William Wilks begins breeding programme to produce 'Shirley poppies' |
| 1883 | *The Daily Telegraph*'s Clement Scott visits Cromer, Norfolk, by train and begins publishing articles, then a poem and eventually *Poppy-land* about it in 1886 |
| 1888 | John Ruskin publishes *Proserpina*, a botanical 'text' featuring the poppy as the perfect flower |

| | |
|---|---|
| 1895 | Heroin first commercially produced, having been produced chemically from morphine in 1874 |
| 1912–19 | International Opium Convention drawn up, leading to worldwide ban on opium trade |
| 1915 | First Remembrance Day; anonymous publication in *Punch* of John McCrae's 'In Flanders Field' |
| 1918 | Moina Michael starts campaign in USA to introduce poppy as symbol of fallen soldiers, taken up in 1920 by USA and other countries in 1921 |
| 1920–24 | Anna Guérin's French war widows make poppy lapels for the world |
| 1924–6 | Earl Haig and Lady Haig set up poppy factories in England and Scotland in 1924 and 1926 respectively |
| 1933 | Women's Cooperative Guild produce white poppy as pacifist protest |
| 1936 | Canon Dick Sheppard forms Peace Pledge Union, adopting white poppy too |
| 1950s–80s | Advent of mass mechanized agriculture and herbicides leads to disappearance of farmland weeds, including poppies, from large areas of countryside |
| 1960s | Irrigation set up in Helmand province, Afghanistan, leading to extensive opium production |
| 1987 | 'Poppy Day massacre' in Enniskillen, Northern Ireland |
| 2006 | MacFarlan Smith start cultivating opium poppies in England<br>Animal Aid issue purple poppies to commemorate animals that died in war |
| 2014 | Centenary of outbreak of First World War, commemorated by installation of 888,246 ceramic poppies around the Tower of London; grants for planting poppies; a commemorative website and several postage stamps depicting poppies |

# References

## 1 What is a Poppy?

1 P. G. Kritikos and S. P. Papadaki, 'The History of the Poppy and of Opium and their Expansion in Antiquity and in the Eastern Mediterranean Area, Part 2', *Bulletin of Narcotics*, XIX (1967), pp. 5–10.

2 J. Bernath, 'Introduction', in *Poppy: The Genus Papaver*, ed. Jeno Bernath (Amsterdam, 1998), pp. 1–6.

3 Geoffrey Grigson, *The Englishman's Flora* (London, 1955).

4 Ibid.

5 P. Wilson and M. King, *Arable Plants: A Field Guide* (Princeton, NJ, 2004).

6 C. D. Preston, D. A. Pearman and T. D. Dines, *New Atlas of the British and Irish Flora* (Oxford, 2002).

7 J. W. Kadereit, 'A Revision of *Papaver* L. section *Rhoeadium* Spach', *Notes Royal Botanic Garden, Edinburgh*, XLV (1989), pp. 225–86.

8 Professor J. W. Kadereit, Johannes Gutenberg Universität, Mainz, personal communication, 2015.

9 R. J. Abbott, J. K. James, J. A. Irwin and H. P. Comes, 'Hybrid Origin of the Oxford Ragwort, *Senecio squalidus* L.', *Watsonia*, XXIII (2000), pp. 123–38.

10 J. W. Kadereit, 'Some Suggestions on the Geographical Origin of the Central, West and North European Synanthropic Species of *Papaver* L.', *Botanical Journal of the Linnean Society*, CIII (1990), pp. 221–31.

11 Richard Mabey, *Flora Britannica* (London, 1996).

## 2 The Poppy Family

1 S. Hoot and P. B. Crane, 'Inter-familial Relationships in the *Ranunculidae* Based on Molecular Systematics', *Plant Systematics and Evolution* [Supplement], IX (1995), pp. 119–31; S. B. Hoot, J. W. Kadereit et al., 'Data Congruence and Phylogeny in Papaveraceae s.l. Based on Four Data Sets *atp*B and *rbc*L Sequences, *trn*K Restriction Sites and Morphological Characters', *Systematic Botany*, XXII (1997), pp. 575–90; H. Sauquet, L. Carrive et al., 'Zygomorphy Evolved

from Dissymmetry in Fumarioideae (Papaveraceae, Ranunculales): New Evidence from an Expanded Molecular Phylogenetic Framework', *Annals of Botany*, 115 (2015), pp. 895–914.

2 Christopher Grey-Wilson, *Poppies: The Poppy Family in the Wild and in Cultivation*, 2nd edn (London, 2005).

3 V. H. Heywood, ed., *Flowering Plant Families of the World* (Oxford, 1978).

4 Grey-Wilson, *Poppies*; Heywood, *Flowering Plant Families*.

5 R.M.M. Crawford, *Tundra-Taiga Biology: Human, Plant and Animal Survival in the Arctic* (Oxford, 2014).

6 Richard Mabey, *Weeds: How Vagabond Plants Gatecrashed Civilisation and Changed the Way We Think About Nature* (London, 2010).

7 See *Papaver rhoeas* 'Shirley Poppy', www.seedaholic.com, accessed 24 November 2015.

8 John Steinbeck, *East of Eden* (New York, 1952).

9 'The Poppy: Golden Blossoms that Greeted the California Pioneers', *Pittsburgh Press*, 2 May 1902, accessed 20 April 2016.

10 Many companies sell tincture of California poppy. See, for instance, 'Through Old Ways Find a New Way' at store.newwayherbs.com.

11 E. E. Smith, *The Golden Poppy* (Palo Alto, CA, 1902).

12 Grey-Wilson, *Poppies*.

13 Ibid.

14 Ibid.

15 J. C. Carolan, I.L.I. Hook, M. W. Chase and J. W. Kadereit, 'Phylogenetics of *Papaver* and Related Genera Based on DNA Sequences from ITS Nuclear Ribosomal DNA and Plastid *trnL* Intron and *trnL-F* Intergenic Spacers', *Annals of Botany*, 98 (2006), pp. 141–55; J. W. Kadereit, C. D. Preston and F. J. Valtueña, 'Is Welsh Poppy, *Meconopsis cambrica* (L.) Vig. (Papaveraceae), Truly a *Meconopsis*?', *New Journal of Botany*, 1 (2011), pp. 80–87.

16 Christopher Grey-Wilson, 'Proposal to Conserve the Name *Meconopsis* (Papaveraceae) with a Conserved Type', *Taxon*, LXI (2012), pp. 473–4.

## 3 The Colour

1 A. Dafni, P. Bernhardt et al., 'Red Bowl-shaped Flowers: Convergence for Beetle Pollination in the Mediterranean', *Israel Journal of Botany*, XXXIX (1990), pp. 81–92.

2 M. Modzelevich, 'Three Sisters: An Israeli Fairy Tale', www.flowersinisrael.com, accessed 24 November 2015.

3 Michael Proctor, Peter Yeo and Andrew Lack, *The Natural History of Pollination* (London, 1996).

4 Dafni, Bernhardt et al., 'Red Bowl-shaped Flowers', pp. 81–92.

5 R. Menzel and A. Schmida, 'The Ecology of Flower Colours and the Natural Colour Vision of Insect Pollinators', *Biological Reviews*, LXVIII (1993), pp. 81–120.

6  Professors R. Menzel, Freie Universität, Berlin and J. Kadereit, Johannes Gutenberg Universität, Mainz, personal communication, 2015.

7  Paul Knuth, *Handbook of Flower Pollination*, trans. J. R. Ainsworth-Davis (Oxford, 1906–9).

8  I. H. McNaughton and J. L. Harper, 'Biological Flora of the British Isles, *Papaver* L.', *Journal of Ecology*, LII (1964), pp. 767–93.

9  Richard Mabey, *Weeds: How Vagabond Plants Gatecrashed Civilisation and Changed the Way We Think About Nature* (London, 2010).

10  C. D. Preston, D. A. Pearman and T. D. Dines, *New Atlas of the British and Irish Flora* (Oxford, 2002).

11  Knuth, *Handbook of Flower Pollination*.

12  Q.O.N. Kay, 'Nectar from Willow Catkins as a Food Source for Blue Tits', *Bird Study*, XXXII (1985), pp. 40–44. Also personal observation.

13  Proctor, Yeo and Lack, *Natural History of Pollination*.

## 4 The Life Cycle of the Poppy

1  Michael Proctor, Peter Yeo and Andrew Lack, *The Natural History of Pollination* (London, 1996).

2  M. J. Lawrence, M. D. Lane, S. O'Donnell and V. E. Franklin-Tonge, 'The Population Genetics of the Self-incompatibility Polymorphism in *Papaver rhoeas*. V. Cross-classification of the S-alleles from Three Natural Populations', *Heredity*, LXXI (1993), pp. 581–90.

3  S. O'Donnell and M. J. Lawrence, 'The Population Genetics of the Self-incompatibility Polymorphism in *Papaver rhoeas*. IV. The Estimation of Numbers of Alleles in a Population', *Heredity*, LIII (1984), pp. 495–507.

4  S. G. Thomas and V. E. Franklin-Tong, 'Self-incompatibility Triggers Programmed Cell Death in *Papaver* Pollen', *Nature*, 429 (2004), pp. 305–9.

5  A. J. Richards, *Plant Breeding Systems*, 2nd edn (London, 1997).

6  Richard Mabey, *Weeds: How Vagabond Plants Gatecrashed Civilisation and Changed the Way We Think About Nature* (London, 2010). Personal observation.

7  Christopher Grey-Wilson, *Poppies: The Poppy Family in the Wild and Cultivation* (London, 2005).

8  See *Papaver rhoeas*, www.kew.org, accessed 27 November 2015; 'Common Poppy', www.gardenorganic.org.uk, 2007.

9  J. Torra and J. Rascens, 'Demography of Corn Poppy (*Papaver rhoeas*) in Relation to Emergence Time and Crop Competition', *Weed Science*, LVI (2008), pp. 826–33; I. H. McNaughton and J. L. Harper, 'Biological Flora of the British Isles, *Papaver* L.', *Journal of Ecology*, LII (1964), pp. 767–93.

## 5 The Poppy as a Symbol of Agriculture

1 K. J. Walker, 'The Last Thirty-five Years: Recent Changes in the Flora of the British Isles', *Watsonia*, XXVI (2007), pp. 291–302.
2 D. E. Balmer, S. Gillings et al., *Bird Atlas, 2007–11* (Thetford, 2013).
3 M. Shoard, *The Theft of the Countryside* (London, 1980); R. Mabey, *The Common Ground* (London, 1980).
4 L. Casswell, 'Herbicide Resistant Poppies Mean Trouble For Growers', *Farmers Weekly*, 5 September 2014.
5 A. Lack, 'Plants', in *Silent Summer*, ed. N. Maclean (Cambridge, 2010), pp. 633–66.
6 Rachel Carson, *Silent Spring* (Cambridge, MA, 1962).
7 D. Buffin and T. Jewell, 'Health and Environmental Impacts of Glyphosate' (Friends of the Earth, 2001); Friends of the Earth Europe, 'The Environmental Impacts of Glyphosate' (Friends of the Earth Europe, 2013).
8 See 'Sumer/Akkadian/Babylonia/Assyria', www.pinterest.com, accessed 27 November 2015; Nicholas J. Saunders, *The Poppy: A History of Conflict, Loss, Remembrance & Redemption* (London, 2013).
9 Robert Graves, *Greek Myths* (London, 1955).
10 There are many references to and pictures of Ceres with poppies around her head. See 'Myths about the Roman Goddess Ceres', www.tribunesandtriumphs.org; 'Ceres', www.talesbeyondbelief.com, both accessed 27 November 2015.
11 Richard Mabey, *Flora Britannica* (London, 1996); Geoffrey Grigson, *The Englishman's Flora* (London, 1955).
12 John Ruskin, *Proserpina: Studies of Wayside Flowers While the Air was Yet Pure Among the Alps and in the Scotland and England that My Father Knew* (London, 1888).
13 E. O. Wilson, *Biophilia* (Cambridge, MA, 1984).
14 D. H. Lawrence, *A Study of Thomas Hardy and Other Essays* [1915] (Cambridge, 1985).
15 D. H. Lawrence, *Reflections on the Death of a Porcupine and Other Essays* [1916] (Cambridge, 1988).

## 6 The Poppy as a Symbol of War and Remembrance

1 There are many sources for statistics on war casualties. The most reliable is probably the *Commonwealth War Graves Commission* Annual Report 2013–14. Also M. Duffy, 'Military Casualties of World War One', www.firstworldwar.com (2009).
2 N. P. Johnson and J. Mueller, 'Updating the Accounts: Global Mortality of the 1918–1920 "Spanish" Influenza Pandemic', *Bulletin of the History of Medicine*, 76 (2002), pp. 105–15. See also '1918 Flu Pandemic', www.history.com, accessed 27 November 2015.

3 Nicholas J. Saunders, *The Poppy: A History of Conflict, Loss, Remembrance and Redemption* (London, 2013).

4 See www.ppu.org.uk, accessed 27 November 2015.

5 Moina Michael, *The Miracle Flower: The Story of the Flanders Fields Memorial Poppy* (Philadelphia, PA, 1941).

6 See www.poppyfactory.org.uk and www.ladyhaigspoppyfactory.org. uk, accessed 27 November 2015.

7 P. Fussell, *The Great War and Modern Memory* (Oxford, 1975).

8 W. Orpen, *An Onlooker in France* (1917–19), quoted by Richard Mabey in *Weeds: How Vagabond Plants Gatecrashed Civilisation and Changed the Way We Think About Nature* (London, 2010).

9 See 'The Story of the Poppy', www.britishlegion.org.uk, accessed 27 November 2015.

10 'BBC revives John Foulds' "A World Requiem for Armistice Day"', 11 November 2007, www.bbc.co.uk.

11 A. Gregory, *The Silence of Memory: Armistice Day, 1918–1946* (London, 1994).

12 See www.ppu.org.uk, accessed 27 November 2015.

13 Vera Brittain, *Born 1925* (London, 1948).

14 See www.cooperativewomensguild.coop, accessed 27 November 2015.

15 See 'Purple Poppy 2011', www.animalaid.org.uk, accessed 27 November 2015.

16 R. Fisk, 'Poppycock', *The Independent*, 7 November 2013.

17 Dan Hodges, 'Wear One, Don't Wear One. It's Time to Call a Truce in the War of the Poppy', *The Daily Telegraph*, 8 November 2013.

18 M. Longley, 'Poppies', in *Collected Poems* (London, 2006).

19 Elyssa Fagan, Paul Cummins Ceramics Ltd, representative, personal communication, 2015.

20 See www.flanderfields1418.com., accessed 10 April 2016.

21 'A Near Observer', *The Battle of Waterloo Part 1: Circumstantial Detail Relative to the Battle of Waterloo*, 8th edn (London, 1816).

22 J. Bate, *John Clare: A Biography* (London, 2004).

23 Lord Macaulay, *A History of England*, Chapter Twenty (London, 1855).

24 'Traveller: The Poppy', *Liverpool Herald*, 19 July 1902.

## 7 Opium

1 J. W. Kadereit, 'A Note on the Genomic Consequences of Regular Bivalent Formation and Continued Fertility in Triploids', *Plant Systematics and Evolution*, CLXXV (1991), pp. 93–9.

2 U. C. Lavania and S. Srivastava, 'Quantitative Delineation of Karyotype Variation in *Papaver* as a Measure of Phylogenetic Differentiation and Origin', *Current Science*, LXXVII (1999), pp. 429–35.

3  A. Aggrawal, *Narcotic Drugs*, Chapter Two (Delhi, 1995); M. J.
   Brownstein, 'A Brief History of Opiates, Opioid Peptides and
   Opioid Receptors', *Proceedings of the National Academy of Sciences*, USA,
   XC (1993), pp. 5391–3; P. G. Kritikos and S. P. Papadaki, 'The History
   of the Poppy and of Opium and their Expansion in Antiquity in
   the Eastern Mediterranean Area' [1967], trans. G. Michalopoulos,
   *Bulletin of Narcotics*, XIX (2001), pp. 17–38.
4  A. N. Hayes and S. J. Gilbert, 'Historical Milestones and Discoveries
   that Shaped the Toxicological Sciences', in *Molecular, Clinical and
   Environmental Toxicology*, vol. I: *Molecular Toxicology*, ed. A. Luch
   (Basel, 2009), pp. 1–35.
5  J. Sawynok, 'The Therapeutic Use of Heroin: A Review of the
   Pharmacological Literature', *Canadian Journal of Physiology and
   Pharmacology*, LXIV (1986), pp. 1–6.
6  MediLexicon International Ltd, 'All About Opioids and Opioid-
   induced Constipation (OIC)', www.medicalnewstoday.com, accessed
   28 November 2015.
7  B. Crosette, 'Taliban's Ban on Poppy a Success, U.S. Aides Say',
   *New York Times*, 20 May 2001.
8  G. Peters, *Seeds of Terror: How Drugs, Thugs and Crime are Reshaping the
   Afghan War* (New York, 2009); R. Nordland, 'Production of Opium
   by Afghans is Up Again', *New York Times*, 15 April 2013.
9  M. D. Merlin, *On the Trail of the Ancient Opium Poppy* (Madison, NJ,
   1985); Pierre-Arnaud Chouvy, *Opium: Uncovering the Politics of the Poppy*
   (London, 2009).
10 B. Ratcliffe, 'Scarab Beetles in Human Culture', *Coleopterists' Society
   Monograph no. 5* (2006), pp. 85–101.
11 N. G. Bisset, J. G. Bruhn et al., 'Was Opium Known in 18th-dynasty
   Ancient Egypt? An Examination of Materials from the Tomb of the
   Chief Royal Architect Kha', *Journal of Ethnopharmacology*, XLI (1994),
   pp. 99–114.
12 E. Astyrakaki, A. Papaioannou and H. Askitopoulou, 'Reference
   to Anesthesia, Pain and Analgesia in the Hippocratic Collection',
   *Anesthetics and Analgesics*, CX (2010), pp. 188–94.
13 J. Bernath and E. Nemeth, 'Poppy: Utilization and Genetic
   Resources', in *Genetic Resources, Chromosome Engineering and Crop
   Improvement*, ed. R. J. Singh, Chapter Fourteen (London, 2012).
14 Kritikos and Papadaki, 'History of the Poppy', pp. 17–38.
15 Aggrawal, *Narcotic Drugs*.
16 H. J. Veitch, 'Nepenthes', *Journal of the Royal Horticultural Society*, XXI
   (1897), pp. 226–62.
17 M. Heydari, M. H. Hashempur and A. Zargaran, 'Medicinal Aspects
   of Opium as Described in Avicenna's Canon of Medicine', *Acta
   Medico-historica Adriatica*, XI (2013), pp. 101–12.
18 Z. Yangwen, *The Social Life of Opium in China* (Cambridge, 2005).
19 P. B. Ebrey, *The Cambridge Illustrated History of China* (Cambridge, 1996).

20  W. T. Hanes III and F. Sanello, *The Opium Wars: The Addiction of One Empire and the Corruption of Another* (Naperville, IL, 2002); J. Lovell, *The Opium War: Drugs, Dreams and the Making of China* (London, 2012).

21  P. Ball, *The Devil's Doctor: Paracelsus and the World of Renaissance Magic and Science* (London, 2006).

22  R. A. Braithwaite, 'Heroin', in *Molecules of Death*, ed. R. H. Waring, G. B. Steventon and S. Mitchell (London, 2007).

23  T. Beddoes, 'Preface' to translation of *The Elements of Medicine of John Brown* (Portsmouth, NH, 1803).

24  Thomas de Quincey, 'Confessions of an English Opium-eater', *London Magazine* (September 1821).

25  N. Roe, *John Keats: A New Life* (New Haven, CT, 2012).

26  A. M. McKinnon, 'Reading "Opium of the People": Expression, Protest and the Dialectics of Religion', *Critical Sociology*, XXXI (2005), pp. 15–38.

27  Oliver Wendell Holmes, 'Currents and Counter-currents in Medical Science' and 'Dr Holmes vs the Medical Profession', address to the Massachusetts Medical Society, 30 May 1860.

28  Nicholas J. Saunders, *The Poppy: A History of Conflict, Loss, Remembrance and Redemption* (London, 2013).

29  L. N. Robins, D. H. Davis and D. W. Goodwin, 'Drug Use by U.S. Army Enlisted Men in Vietnam: A Follow-up on their Return Home', *American Journal of Epidemiology*, XCIX (1973), pp. 235–49; James Clear, 'Breaking Bad Habits: How Vietnam War Veterans Broke their Heroin Addictions', www.jamesclear.com, accessed 29 November 2015.

30  G. Peters, *Seeds of Terror* (New York, 2009).

31  K. Thodey, S. Galanie and C. D. Smolke, 'A Microbial Biomanufacturing Platform for Natural and Semisynthetic Opioids', *Nature Chemical Biology*, X (2014), pp. 837–44.

## 8 Other Uses and Associations

1  Food and Agriculture Organization of the United Nations Statistics Division, faostat3.fao.org, accessed 29 November 2015.

2  Ibid.

3  P. L. Vincent, 'Import of Turkish White Poppy Seeds Threaten Opium Farmers', *The Hindu*, 18 January 2014.

4  L. Ekici, 'Effects of Concentration Methods on Bioactivity and Color Properties of Poppy (*Papaver rhoeas* L.) Sorbet, a Traditional Turkish Beverage', LWT *Food Science and Technology*, 56 (2014), pp. 40–48.

5  See 'Adagelincik Red Poppy', www.bozcaada.info, accessed 29 November 2015; Jennie McCabe, personal communication, 2015.

6  See 'Poppyseed Oil: A Rare Almost Forgotten Oil', www.bioplanete.com, accessed 29 November 2015.

7 R. E. Hind, M. Loizidou et al., 'Biodistribution of Lipiodol Following Hepatic Arterial Injection', *European Journal of Surgical Oncology*, 18 (1992), pp. 162–7.

8 B. Creevy, *The Oil Painting Book: Materials and Techniques for Today's Artists* (New York, 1994).

9 Margaret Thatcher, 'Speech to the Institute of SocioEconomic Studies, "Let Our Children Grow Tall"', 15 September 1975, www.margaretthatcher.org, accessed 29 November 2015.

10 'Tall-poppy syndrome', www.users.tinyonline.co.uk/gswithenbank/sayingst.htm, accessed 29 November 2015.

11 P. Hartcher, 'Voters Now at Ease with Rich Pickings', *Sydney Morning Herald*, 30 July 2013.

12 J. Allen, *Lost Geographies of Power* (Oxford, 2003).

13 See Simon Appleyard, 'Poppyland', from *This England* (1987), http://jermy.org, accessed 29 November 2015.

14 C. Scott, *Poppy-land: Papers Descriptive of Scenery on the East Coast* (Norwich, 1886); D. Cleveland, 'Poppy-land', *The Lady* (5 June 1975), pp. 1002–3. See 'Poppyland', www.literarynorfolk.co.uk, and 'A Dictionary of Cromer and Overstrand History', www.cromerdictionary.co.uk, accessed 12 November 2015.

15 F. D. Bergen, 'Poppy Shows', *Journal of American Folklore*, 8 (1895), pp. 152–3.

16 See Mercedé K., 'Poppy Field in Mt Damavand', http://under-cloudy-sky.blogspot.co.uk, 3 April 2012; '*Papaver rhoeas*', en.wikipedia.org, accessed 12 November 2015.

17 See K. Edley, '*Argemone Mexicana* – Prickly Poppy', www.entheology.org, accessed 29 November 2015.

18 Michael Longley, 'A Poppy', from *Collected Poems* (London, 2006).

# Further Reading

The poppy is mentioned in many different types of literature, from botanical descriptions to symbols, associations and novels. The novels are excluded from this list. All of these books are referred to in the text where relevant.

Bernath, Jeno, *Poppy: The Genus Papaver* (Amsterdam, 1998)
Chouvy, Pierre-Arnaud, *Opium: Uncovering the Politics of the Poppy* (London, 2009)
de Quincey, Thomas, 'Confessions of an English Opium-eater' (London, 1821)
Grey-Wilson, Christopher, *Poppies: The Poppy Family in the Wild and Cultivation*, 2nd edn (London, 2005)
Grigson, Geoffrey, *The Englishman's Flora* (London, 1955)
Knuth, Paul, *Handbook of Flower Pollination*, trans. J. R. Ainsworth-Davis (Oxford, 1906–9)
Mabey, Richard, *Flora Britannica* (London, 1996)
—, *Weeds: How Vagabond Plants Gatecrashed Civilisation and Changed the Way We Think About Nature* (London, 2010)
McNab, Chris, *The Book of the Poppy* (Stroud, 2014)
Michael, Moina, *The Miracle Flower: The Story of the Flanders Fields Memorial Poppy* (Philadelphia, 1941)
Preston, C. D., D. A. Pearman and T. D. Dines, *New Atlas of the British and Irish Flora* (Oxford, 2002)
Proctor, Michael, Peter Yeo and Andrew Lack, *The Natural History of Pollination* (London, 1996)
Ruskin, John, *Proserpina: Studies of Wayside Flowers While the Air was Yet Pure Among the Alps and in the Scotland and England that My Father Knew* (London, 1888)
Saunders, Nicholas J., *The Poppy: A History of Conflict, Loss, Remembrance and Redemption* (London, 2013)
Scott, Clement, *Poppy-land: Papers Descriptive of Scenery on the East Coast* (Norwich, 1886)

# Associations and Websites

General sources such as Wikipedia can be an excellent first source for information. Poppies are mentioned in floras and gardening societies from countries across the world. For associations with the poppy in horticulture, see especially:

THE ROYAL BOTANIC GARDENS, KEW
www.kew.org

THE ROYAL HORTICULTURAL SOCIETY
Based at Wisley and elsewhere in the UK.
www.rhs.org.uk

For associations with the poppy as a symbol of war:

THE ROYAL BRITISH LEGION
Their poppies are produced in two poppy factories,
see www.poppyfactory.org.uk and
www.ladyhaigspoppyfactory.org.uk.
www.britishlegion.org.uk

REMEMBRANCE TRAVEL
The travel website for the Royal British Legion.
www.remembrancetravel.org.uk
www.firstworldwar.com

Other associations include:

ANIMAL AID
www.animalaid.org.uk.

THE PEACE PLEDGE UNION
www.ppu.org.uk

POPPY LAND, NORFOLK
See www.literarynorfolk.co.uk and www.cromerdictionary.co.uk

THE WOMEN'S COOPERATIVE GUILD
www.cooperativewomensguild.coop

More websites are cited in the reference list and many other references cited for the individual chapters can be accessed online.

# Acknowledgements

My thanks to Hugh Warwick who first suggested to my editor, Michael Leaman, that I write this book. Michael has given me the leeway to do much of it in my own way and he has provided encouragement, suggestions and comments throughout. Martha Jay has helped it through the final stages. Rien de Keyser, Lesley Maudsley, Michael Proctor and Steven Pollock have generously given me permission to use their excellent photographs. The book has benefited considerably from correspondence with Professor Joachim Kadereit with insight from his long-term studies on poppies, and he and Professor Randolf Menzel provided the photographs of ultraviolet reflectance patterns. My daughter, Jennie McCabe, celebrated her wedding in Turkey and could tell me at first hand about the Turkish connection with poppies. Elyssa Fagan of Paul Cummins Ceramics Ltd provided information about Cummins's magnificent installation at the Tower of London. Professor Sharon Ruston guided me to the story about John Brown and opium. Chris Holdsworth led me to the context of the quote by Marx. My wife, Helen, read the book at various stages of completion and, as ever, has provided numerous useful comments as well as the vital back-up of family life. To all these people I am most grateful.

PERMISSION
For permission to quote James Stephens, 'In the Poppy Field', © The Society of Authors as the Literary Representative of the Estate of James Stephens.

For permission to quote Michael Longley, 'A Poppy' and 'Poppies', from *Collected Poems* by Michael Longley, published by Jonathan Cape. Reproduced by permission of The Random House Group Ltd

# Photo Acknowledgements

The author and publishers wish to express their thanks to the below sources of illustrative material and/or permission to reproduce it. Some locations of artworks are also given below, in the interests of brevity.

Photo Adrian198cm: p. 21 (left); Art Institute of Chicago: p. 91 (top); Ashmolean Museum, University of Oxford: p. 88; Austrian National Library, Vienna: p. 43; photos courtesy of the author: pp. 9, 22, 23, 25, 28, 34, 36, 37, 42, 49, 50, 52 (top), 61, 63, 66, 68, 71, 76, 77, 78, 105, 118, 119, 121, 132; from Elizabeth Blackwell, *A Curious Herbal, Containing Five Hundred Cuts, of the Most Useful Plants, which are now Used in the Practice of Physick*... (London, 1737): p. 10; photo Bobdatty: p. 107; British Museum, London: p. 131; Cpl Max Bryan/MOD, the copyright holder of the photo on pp. 110–11, and Mike Weston ABIPP/MOD, the copyright holder of the image on p. 103, have published these under the Open Government Licence v1.0 [OGL] – readers are free to copy, publish, distribute and transmit the Information – adapt the Information – exploit the Information commercially for example, by combining it with other Information, or by including it in their own product or application – but readers must, where they do any of the above, acknowledge the source of the Information by including any attribution statement specified by the Information Provider(s) and, where possible, provide a link to this licence – ensure that they do not use the Information in a way that suggests any official status or that the Information Provider endorses them or their use of the Information – ensure that they do not mislead others or misrepresent the Information or its source – and ensure that their use of the Information does not breach the Data Protection Act 1998 or the Privacy and Electronic Communications [EC Directive] Regulations 2003); from Joseph-Pierre Buch'oz, *Collection précieuse et enluminée des fleurs les plus belles et les plus curieuses* ... (Paris, 1776): p. 46; photo caviarkirch: p. 149; photo Daderot: p. 144; photo Rien de Keyser: p. 6; from J.-N. de la Hire, *Plantes du jardin royal etably à Paris représentées au naturel par une nouvelle pratique de dessine Inventée et executée par Jean-Nicolas de La Hire*... vol. IV (Paris, 1715–1720): p. 43; Gemeentemuseum Den Haag, Netherlands: p. 92; from John Gerard, *Herball, or Generall Historie of Plantes* (London, 1597): p. 57; Herakleion Archaeological Museum, Herakleion, Crete: p. 140;

photo javier martin: p. 26; photo KGM007: p. 135; photo Library of Congress, Washington, DC (Prints and Photographs Division): p. 166; photo Nerijus Liulys: p. 8; Los Angeles Museum of Contemporary Art (www.lacma.org – Charles H. Quinn Bequest (75.4.9)): p. 32; photos Lesley Maudsley: pp. 124, 125; photo Ricardo Mertsch: p. 164; Metropolitan Museum of Art: pp. 15, 38, 53, 86; photo Mpv_51: p. 135; Musée du Louvre, Paris (photo Marie-Lan Nguyen): p. 82; Musée d'Orsay, Paris: p. 91 (foot); Museo Pio Clementino, Rome: p. 83; National Museum of Vietnamese History, Hanoi, Vietnam: p. 144; photo Nina Sean Feenan: p. 115; Peace Pledge Union: p. 113; photo Steven Pollock: p. 176; private collections: pp. 146, 169; photo Michael Proctor: p. 45; from Pierre-Joseph Redoute, *Choix des plus belles fleurs . . .* (Paris, 1827–34): p. 130; photo Shakko: p. 169; from Edward Step, *Favourite Flowers of Garden and Greenhouse*, pictures by D. Bois, vol. 1 (London, 1896): p. 73; photo Taylor S-K (National Library of Scotland): p. 104; photo The Marzipan Duck: p. 155; from O. W. Thome, *Flora von Deutschland, Osterreich und der Schweiz . . .* (Berlin, 1885): p. 11; photo Topjabot: p. 11; photo United States Marine Corps: p. 161; U.S. Post Office Department: p. 107; photo xQGTinA-MPxcVg: p. 91 (foot).

BioDivLibrary, the copyright holder of the photo on p. 173; docentjoyce, the copyright holder of the photo on p. 41; mari27454, the copyright holder of the photo on p. 84; Simon Mortimer, the copyright holder of the photo on p. 137; Björn S . . ., the copyright holder of the photo on p. 20; sybarite48, the copyright holder of the photo on p. 24; Thoth, God of Knowledge, the copyright holder of the photo on p. 99; and vintage dept, the copyright holder of the photo on p. 140, have published these online under conditions imposed by a Creative Commons Attribution 2.0 Generic license. William Avery, the copyright holder of the photo on p. 142; Wknight94, the copyright holder of the photo on p. 83; Etan f, the copyright holder of the photo on p. 17, Gzhao, the copyright holder of the photo on p. 44; C T Johansson, the copyright holder of the photo on p. 52; and SuperJw, the copyright holder of the photo p. 62, have published these online under conditions imposed by a Creative Commons Attribution 3.0 Unported license. Fæ, the copyright holder of the photo on p. 151; and Isidre blanc, the copyright holder of the photo on p. 21, have published these online under conditions imposed by a Creative Commons Attribution-Share Alike 4.0 International license. Wuzur, the copyright holder of the photo on pp. 30–31, has published this online under conditions imposed by a Creative Commons Attribution-Share Alike 3.0 Unported, 2.5 Generic, 2.0 Generic and 1.0 Generic license.

any reader is free to share – to copy, distribute and transmit the work, or to remix – to adapt the work, under the following conditions: you must give appropriate credit, provide a link to the license, and indicate if changes were made – you may do so in any reasonable manner, but not in any way that suggests the licensor endorses you or your use – with no additional restrictions – you may not apply legal terms or technological measures that legally restrict others from doing anything the license permits.

# Index

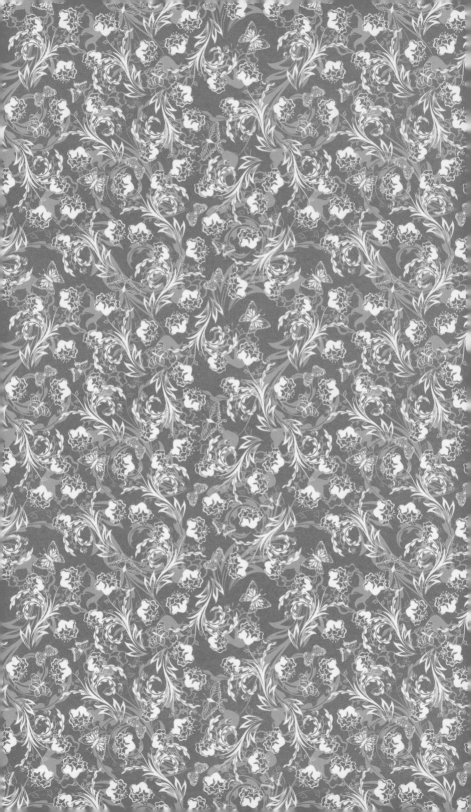